A Path with Psychedelics

A
Path
with
Psychedelics

A Journal of Journeys

CHRIS BECKER

Publisher: True Way Press; Berkeley, California

道真

For further information visit: https://www.chrisbecker.org/

Cover design by Tanja Prokop (Bookcoverworld.com)

Formatting & typesetting by Graciela Kinkela

Library of Congress Control Number: 2024902938

ISBN (paperback): 979-8-9901026-0-6

ISBN (ebook): 979-8-9901026-1-3

ISBN (audiobook): 979-8-9901026-2-0

First Edition: 2024.

To the ancestors, past and future:
honoring your sacrifices, wisdom and compassion.

THE GUEST HOUSE

This being human is a guest house.
Every morning a new arrival.

A joy, a depression, a meanness,
some momentary awareness comes
as an unexpected visitor.

Welcome and entertain them all!
Even if they're a crowd of sorrows,
who violently sweep your house
empty of its furniture,
still, treat each guest honorably.
He may be clearing you out
for some new delight.

The dark thought, the shame, the malice,
meet them at the door laughing,
and invite them in.

Be grateful for whoever comes,
because each has been sent
as a guide from beyond.

by Jalaluddin Rumi
Tr. Coleman Barks

CONTENTS

POEMS

ACKNOWLEDGMENTS

With gratitude and love for my family and friends. Special thanks to my guide-therapist, who skillfully helped me along this path. With appreciation for Alex Theberge, LMFT, who served as my initial kindhearted "above-ground" therapist. And last but certainly not least, thanks go to my editor, Emily Moberg Robinson, for her insightful and caring craft.

INTRODUCTION

A Path with Psychedelics: A Journal of Journeys describes a path of psychic healing and spiritual growth. Just one path: my path. Each person's path is unique; and yet each life path has elements in common with others, especially for seekers of healing and spiritual connection. Just as every river has its own distinctive twists and turns, every river also runs downhill, between its banks and to the sea. A river may be hugely twisted or even subterranean, but nevertheless, it flows. And as the song says, the ocean refuses no river. In any case, I believe there is value in examining one person's path in some detail as a guide to the what and the how of the universal human journey. That's why I am offering up my story.

Psychedelics play a central role in this work, but this work isn't only about psychedelics. It's about my journey to heal the sacred wounding I received as a child, to grow and mature as a person, and to open to the spiritual realm. Psychedelics are a special kind of medicine, helping substances. Yet it's my own nature, my own internal wisdom, that propels me forward—and I wholeheartedly believe that *everyone* has this capacity to propel themselves forward.

My path began primarily with psychedelic-assisted therapy, and then opened more toward spiritual growth. The path is complex and nonlinear.

To better appreciate the process of healing, it is useful to first reflect on the nature and causes of suffering and the many types of injuries humans encounter. I discuss the origins and impacts of trauma, especially childhood trauma, in chapter 1. In addition, I include two other short essays in this collection: I reflect on the intrinsic duality of nature in chapter 5, and on ego death in chapter 8.

In the rest of this monograph, I describe and analyze the many journeys that I have undertaken in the past several years, narrating them in chronological order. Chapters begin with the intentions I set beforehand, followed by a brief description of the setting, any notes that my guide recorded from my speaking, a description of the journey itself, and commentary. Each chapter concludes with a photograph, drawing, or poem, my work unless otherwise noted.

Rather than just reading a collection of "trip reports," I hope you will encounter the flow of a river of healing and growth. I discussed my first few journeys in my previous book, *Healing with Psychedelics: Essays and Poems on Spirituality and Transformation,* but a new perspective emerges here.

Although this book focuses on the medicine journeys themselves, it is important to keep in mind that for the first year and a half of my work, I was also having weekly Hakomi-method somatic therapy sessions with my guide, meditating daily, and doing other work supporting the integration of the journeys into my life.

For most of the approaches employed in conventional psychotherapy, including Hakomi, the goal is to bring unconscious material into conscious awareness where it can be understood and worked with for a healing effect. Psychedelic-assisted psychotherapy does this, too, but at a much-accelerated pace. One of the reasons to have a well-trained therapist-guide is to get help in making this rapid process manageable, safe, and long-lasting.

However, working with psychedelics offers considerably more than accelerated healing. It offers new experiences and wisdom that are difficult to attain through other methods like meditation. These are profound, peak experiences, like vistas seen from mountain peaks.

For example, there are experiences where a journeyer feels wonder, joy, and peace, giving them a taste of what true health is like. These journeys provide new perspectives and a greater understanding of the potentials of life, a compass to assist the journeyer to find their path to a higher love. Wisdom and compassion take deeper root.

Other experiences are of a spiritual nature, where the journeyer communes with Divine Light or spirits of different sorts. There can be transpersonal experiences, and opportunities for healing intergenerational trauma. Sometimes the sense of self (ego) is left behind in what is called ego death or non-dual awareness. This is helpful for understanding that our sense of self—our body, intellect, and emotions—is transitory. We are really spirit, soul, pure consciousness; this body is only a temporary garment.

But what a garment! To be sure, it comes from dust and goes to dust. But in between? This garment is no lifeless thing. It can learn, not just walk and talk. It can love; it can feel joy, sadness, grief. It is enlivened, it is imbued with spirit, and, it appears, it is a vehicle in which our spirit develops. Perhaps the key question is: Is everything, including this body, spirit? In other words, as the Buddhists say, is form emptiness, emptiness form? Our human form, if nothing else, is an embodiment of the Great Mystery.

1

The Origin and Nature of Human Suffering

Suffering. What could be a bigger, more important subject? Thousands of scriptures, poems, and books reflect on the topic. It's so consequential that even a major world religion has human suffering as its underpinning.

In Buddhism, the first of the four noble truths is that life is suffering. The second truth is that suffering is caused by grasping or desire or attachment, together with delusion or ignorance. One can argue that delusion, an incorrect perception or understanding of reality, is the root cause of grasping, but no need to parse that here.

The third noble truth is that there exists a release from this suffering, a concept sometimes described as *nirvana*. And the fourth noble truth lays out the way to achieve this release: the eightfold path of right view, right intention, right speech, right action, right livelihood, right effort, right mindfulness, and right concentration. No doubt all good and helpful, but a little nebulous, too. For starters, how do you know if you have the right view of reality?

Although no one can claim to absolutely know the true nature of reality or the fundamental cause of suffering, we each can have our opinions and beliefs. I believe, as do others, that the foundational cause of human suffering is the delusion that we are only our bodies and our egos, instead of perceiving ourselves as truly spirit and part of one Great Spirit. This does not mean that our bodies aren't also spirit. Perhaps better said: the problem is not realizing that the physical is also the spiritual, believing that the physical we normally perceive is all there is, and convincing ourselves that we are separate from the rest of divinity. Whew! Maybe *best* said: the nature of reality is the Great Mystery.

I believe these Buddhist teachings point to truth, and that the eightfold path is to be respected. However, they also can feel esoteric, rarefied, abstract. There are more concrete descriptions about human nature and the human condition that help us understand suffering—and help us find relief.

Kinds of Suffering

This writing is largely concerned with psychological suffering, or psychic suffering, or the anguish of the soul, especially (although not exclusively) in the earlier chapters. *The Diagnostic and Statistical Manual of Mental Disorders (DSM)* lists many kinds of mental disorders–and the fifth edition is over 1,000 pages long. Even given the legitimate criticisms of the *DSM*, there can be no argument that psychological disturbances surface in many different ways. And often, physical suffering (diseases and other physical maladies) accompanies psychological suffering. In fact, some scholars, like physician and author Gabor Maté, argue that most physical maladies originate in a pain-filled and struggling psyche. There is ample data to support this argument.

Psychological problems most often originate in infancy and childhood. To be sure, severe issues do originate from discrete traumas. Sometimes called Type I or acute trauma, they include events like warfare, natural disasters, physical and sexual assaults, and automobile accidents. But childhood developmental traumas (Type II, or chronic) are extremely common, and cause lifelong pain and dysfunctional behavioral strategies.

Although this work is also relevant to adult trauma, this chapter examines in particular what can and does go wrong during childhood. The focus on developmental trauma will help contextualize my own healing path, allowing readers to extrapolate my healing work to their own situations as appropriate.

Developmental Trauma and Adverse Childhood Experiences (ACEs)

Although sudden, terrible events can occur during childhood, childhood trauma generally is repetitive and occurs over an extended period of time. Some of these traumas are more easily recognized than others, but we should be cautioned against judging one type of trauma as more severe than another. There can be so many unseen factors.

I've read that simple emotional neglect is one of the most profoundly injurious types of trauma. I believe this is true. It is hard to quantify. In fact, an adult may have no recollection of the recurring disapproving look a parent gave them when they acted in a way the parent didn't like—or perhaps even worse, of the times their parent looked away when the child was seeking their gaze. Withholding acknowledgment when a child is seeking approval can be crushing; it feels like a total rejection, and the child interprets it as showing there is something wrong with them. What can be worse than isolation, abandonment in any form? After all, the worst punishment in a prison is solitary confinement. A child will do anything to feel connected and cared for and loved, even changing who they are. This survival strategy becomes a key part of their personality that they come to accept as their intrinsic makeup. Fortunately, with healing work, these masks can be removed.

Nevertheless, it is useful to start this overview with specific types of identifiable traumas, sometimes called "adverse childhood experiences" or ACEs. I've written about ACEs in my prior book, but some of these facts bear repeating.

The United States Centers for Disease Control (CDC) has determined that most of you reading this have or will have a serious illness that will last for many years, if not the remainder of your life. It may quite likely result in your early death. Your physician has no cure for you; there is no drug to lessen your suffering. I'm referring, of course, to childhood trauma, described by CDC as "adverse childhood experiences."[1] Most people haven't heard of ACEs, even though they are the largest contributing factor to disease and sickness in this country. According to CDC, ACEs encompass any abuse, neglect, and other trauma experienced by people under the age of 18. These can take many forms. Physical abuse includes, among other things, hitting, kicking, and shaking. Sexual abuse includes pressuring or forcing a child to engage in sexual acts, or exposing them to a range of sexual activities. Emotional abuse is behavior that damages a child's emotional well-being and sense of self-worth; this may include actual abandonment, threats of abandonment or violence, shaming, name calling, withholding love and physical affection, or other forms of psychological maltreatment. Neglect is the failure to meet a child's physical and emotional needs for things like proper housing, medical care, food, and clothing. Other examples of ACEs include witnessing violence against a mother or stepmother; substance abuse by a parent or other household member; mental illness suffered by a family member; a suicide attempt by or death of a parent or other household member; the incarceration of a parent or other household member; and parental separation or divorce.

Many children suffer very severe ACEs during their pre-memory and/or pre-verbal stages of life, before they turn four years old. Moreover, while an ACE can be a single traumatic event that happens on a particular day, ACEs also can last

---

1   https://www.cdc.gov/violenceprevention/aces/

weeks, months, or years. In fact, a great majority of the children who have one ACE go on to experience multiple adverse events—87%, by one research estimate.

In 1998, CDC and Kaiser Permanente jointly published the first study on ACEs, using the confidential survey data of 17,000 mostly white, middle-class, college-educated adults in Southern California. Since then, physicians and psychologists have published more than 2,000 peer-reviewed studies on the causes and effects of Adverse Childhood Experiences. This research has demonstrated that the majority of people living in the United States have suffered one or more significant adverse childhood experiences. An estimated two thirds of us have been unloved or otherwise injured when we were defenseless children—and this two thirds may even be an underestimate.

The consequences of Adverse Childhood Experiences are long lasting, often persisting throughout an individual's entire life. ACEs are linked to early death, chronic health conditions, risky health behaviors, and a variety of psychological maladies. Research has shown that ACEs lead to much higher rates of cancer, diabetes, and heart disease, depression, anxiety, suicide, and other mental afflictions, as well as alcohol and drug abuse, smoking, and other forms of addictive behavior.

So far, I've been speaking about the consequences of ACEs for individuals. But children grow up and enter platonic, familial, and romantic relationships. What about these relationships? You can guess—it's not a good story. Think about divorce rates, for example. And who's not talking to whom, or who's yelling at whom.

Briefly, people who have suffered traumatic experiences during their childhood often end up with what is known as insecure or anxious attachment style, "a relationship style where the bond is contaminated by fear" (exploringyourmind.com). As adults, they find it difficult to trust and be intimate with others; this leads to unstable relationships, especially romantic relationships. Depression, anxiety, and substance abuse and other addictions also interfere with maintaining healthy relationships. These maladaptive behaviors are driven from deep within the unconscious mind, formed during childhood exposure to ACEs.

Calling this a public health crisis is not an exaggeration. And if two thirds or more of you reading this have suffered ACEs, as research has established, then what? If you aren't already aware of your past in this regard, a first step is to take an ACE questionnaire to help learn more about your own childhood experiences and how they may be affecting you today. A copy of the questionnaire can be found at the end of this chapter, as well as online.[2]

While the questionnaire is truly valuable, it does have limitations. Many childhood traumas occur pre-memory or are repressed—they are not easily accessed. Additionally, some

---

2   For example, the National Council of Juvenile and Family Court Judges has published the questionnaire on its website: www.ncjfcj.org/wp-content/uploads/2006/10/Finding-Your-Ace-Score.pdf

A Path with Psychedelics

traumatic experiences are too subtle to generate a score on the questionnaire, and may not necessarily have been incurred through someone's conscious or purposeful action (although in some cases, they may have been deliberately inflicted). However, even these subtle experiences can undermine your belief that you were valued or welcomed in the world as you truly are.

It is fitting that CDC, which is well known for its work on communicable diseases like COVID-19, is researching and tracking ACEs. Childhood trauma is passed down from generation to generation, whether by behavior, epigenetics, or some other mechanism. Given the high prevalence of ACEs in the United States, calling this an epidemic is appropriate. It's an epidemic that has been present for centuries, if not millennia. And identifying your ACEs is the first step to breaking the intergenerational cycle that perpetuates the problem.

The Universal Separation

Even for those of us who had attentive, skillful, and loving parents or caregivers, life is not nirvana. We still struggle with anxieties, disappointments, the loss of loved ones and dear things, and so on. Having stellar parents and not experiencing acute trauma are undoubtedly blessings, but that is not a remedy for all woes.

All of us experience some separation that causes suffering in one way or another. This is a primary premise of this book:

being and feeling separated from loved ones and a supportive community is naturally painful. It is a universal human experience. We are social animals. Separation and isolation are painful and destabilizing.

How are we separated? Separation can happen in multiple ways. Let's start with birth. Some thought leaders, like Stanislav Grof, argue that the birth process itself, even in a "smooth" delivery, constitutes a great trauma event for the baby human, a trauma that generally remains even after reaching adulthood. (Grof has written about treating birth trauma with LSD-assisted therapies.) It certainly makes sense, doesn't it? The baby is safe and warm inside its mother's womb, and then is expelled into a completely foreign environment, forced to breathe on its own and experience hunger pains and other bodily discomforts. This expulsion conjures up the story of the Garden of Eden, in which Adam and Eve were expelled from paradise.

Problems mount after birth. There is a natural desire to be satisfied. The baby and young child is naturally narcissistic. No matter how attentive the caregivers are, their needs are never fully met. At some point in childhood, the child realizes that its desires are impossible to satisfy, and a search for compensating strategies takes hold. These coping strategies, also called traits, personalities, or character types, manifest well into adulthood and usually are taken to the grave. Hakomi psychotherapy, a practice I'm especially familiar with, lists eight common compensating strategies; naturally there are spectrums within and blendings among them. Part of this psychological landscape is the early childhood attachment style; attachment theory is truly useful in understanding child and adult behavior. But even a "securely attached" adult knows the world is precarious and inherently unstable, experienced in a body that is fundamentally separate and destined for destruction. I don't want to write an exposé here on this incredibly large topic. To speak simply: life is challenging and scary at best and horrendous at worst, and the child-to-adult does the best they can to survive and seek out whatever happiness they can find. No one escapes unscathed.

On top of all this, the environment has a large impact on both child development and adult psychic health. Many would argue that we live in a toxic society, dealing with the stress of capitalism, the fear of growing old and penniless, political divisiveness, hate, fear mongers, crime... and more! But back to the Garden of Eden. (Wouldn't that be sweet!) There's another important reading of this biblical fable: it chronicles the development (dare we say, evolution?) of human consciousness, that elevated self-awareness that makes our psyche especially... hmmm, shall we say, *tricky*? And the fable itself is a good example. Eve is the guilty party causing the expulsion. So out of the Garden of Eden springs not only human self-awareness, but also misogyny! Pretty tricky, eh?

What this Path is About

My particular path initially was mostly focused on healing my wounds and sense of separation. I did this by revisiting my woundings with self-compassion, with the help of powerful medicines, and in the presence of another loving human being and spirit. The wounding, and thus the healing, does not reside primarily in the frontal cortex of the brain. It resides as well, somehow, in the body and spirit. That's why conventional talk therapy by itself often is not completely effective, although it can be helpful.

As part of the healing process, with or without any psychedelic medicine, it is useful to employ mindfulness when working with our psyche, our consciousness. Mindfulness is observing whatever experience we are having without judging, paying attention to the here and now without wishing things were different.

The big picture? Unity. Unconditional love. That is the direction and guiding force of the path. Healing is on the path. Spiritual growth is on the path. Helping others is on the path.

Finding Your ACE Score

While you were growing up, during your first 18 years of life:

1. Did a parent or other adult in the household often or very often... Swear at you, insult you, put you down, or humiliate you? or
   Act in a way that made you afraid that you might be physically hurt?

   Yes   No   If yes enter 1 _____

2. Did a parent or other adult in the household often or very often... Push, grab, slap, or throw something at you? or
   Ever hit you so hard that you had marks or were injured?

   Yes   No   If yes enter 1 _____

3. Did an adult or person at least 5 years older than you ever...
   Touch or fondle you or have you touch their body in a sexual way? or
   Attempt or actually have oral, anal, or vaginal intercourse with you?

   Yes   No   If yes enter 1 _____

4. Did you often or very often feel that ...
   No one in your family loved you or thought you were important or special? or
   Your family didn't look out for each other, feel close to each other, or support each other?

   Yes   No   If yes enter 1 _____

5. Did you often or very often feel that ...
   You didn't have enough to eat, had to wear dirty clothes, and had no one to protect you? or
   Your parents were too drunk or high to take care of you or take you to the doctor if you needed it?

   Yes   No   If yes enter 1 _____

6. Were your parents ever separated or divorced?

   Yes   No   If yes enter 1 _____

7. Was your mother or stepmother:
   Often or very often pushed, grabbed, slapped, or had something thrown at her? or
   Sometimes, often, or very often kicked, bitten, hit with a fist, or hit with something hard? or
   Ever repeatedly hit at least a few minutes or threatened with a gun or knife?

   Yes   No   If yes enter 1 _____

8. Did you live with anyone who was a problem drinker or alcoholic or who used street drugs?

   Yes   No   If yes enter 1 _____

9. Was a household member depressed or mentally ill, or did a household member attempt suicide?

   Yes   No   If yes enter 1 _____

10. Did a household member go to prison?

    Yes   No   If yes enter 1 _____

Now add up your "Yes" answers: _____ This is your ACE Score.

Adapted from: http://www.acestudy.org/files/ACE_Score_Calculator.pdf, 092406RA4CR

THE BASEMENT

Descent into the basement,
unwilling, pushed down there
as a child by a sadistic father.
How to make sense of that?
Who would do that?

A broken soul?
Is that where evil lives, escapes?
How broken? Why broken?

What is the origin of evil?
Is there such a thing?
Hard to understand

When smooth pottery breaks,
the edges are sharp.
Was the sharpness there all along?
Is evil like that?

Canines are sharp.
Meat eaters have them,
humans have them.
What does that mean?

God is love.
God is everything
scriptures say

So God has canines?
And growls and rips flesh?
And has guns that shoot children?
Locks them in basements?

Time for faith and love.
Pray for healing,
work for healing

2

MDMA Journey, January 2019

Intentions

Visit my early childhood: Looking for love and physical affection. Associated loneliness, sadness.

Forgive parents.

Alcohol use: what did it fulfill?

Commune with the source. Let go. Feel gratitude, and loving kindness.

Setting

A room in a house in a residential neighborhood; the San Francisco Bay Area. A thin but comfortable mattress placed in the middle of the room; a blanket, a pillow with an eye mask. A nearby altar holding my intentions written on a piece of paper and a handful of photos from my childhood. Music playing.

From my guide's notes

I'm feeling the pain my parents had. Their unhappy marriage. Compassion for them. They didn't love each other, at least when I knew them. And they didn't or couldn't love their children. My mother was angry at her father and didn't love men. Was unhappy having three sons.

[while in child state] Lonely. Wondering about the world, what does it all mean? Needing to explore.

[while in adult state] Wondering about other children. No joy. I found joy with dogs, brother. My mother was absent. I'm looking for whatever feels good. Alcohol. To numb the pain. Loneliness. I looked to my brother. He was angry and took it out on me.

[in childhood bedroom, shifting between child and adult view] I just look at the ceiling.

It's hard to give love if you've never had it. I tried hard for my kids, held them. They love me.

I'm not used to love, no training in it.

Alcohol, it's nursing the pain. Feels warm; pot, too.

I can open up now. I understand why I cried the first day of school when lining up at the door to go home. I always wanted to find out.

Journey

This was my first journey in decades. Back in my twenties, I had multiple experiences with peyote and LSD, and one time with magic mushrooms. Maybe MDMA or something similar, once—not sure. That didn't matter now. That was long ago; four decades had passed. Basically, everything felt new. I was excited to begin this journey and to make positive changes in my life, notably refraining without struggle from alcohol and cannabis, and learning about and healing from trauma in my early childhood. Although drinking alcohol was and is very concrete, the talk psychotherapy leading up to the day—all of a couple months—was showing me that this path was not really about alcohol. Alcohol abuse was just a symptom of something bigger.

I would be in this same room quite a number of times over the next few years. Today, an altar was set up holding an eclectic collection of articles: a few American and Mexican Indian objects, some feathered; a Virgin of Guadalupe candle, Tibetan bowls, some shells, driftwood, a Hindu love sculpture, and two other small sculptures. Nearby, there was a two-foot-tall lovely wooden Buddha sculpture. Reflective of the new focus on my early life, I brought a handful of photos from my childhood, some of just me and a couple with my parents. My guide and I looked at them together, and I shared what they revealed about the three of us. I placed the pictures on the altar, too. The guide played supportive recorded music through speakers in the room.

After this check-in, my guide began the session with a ceremonial sage smudging of both of us, followed by a prayer. Then, as was his custom, he left me alone with the medicine, stepping out for about fifteen or twenty minutes. This gave me time to focus on my intentions, be with the medicine, say a prayer, and/or just relax.

The MDMA was a high-purity crystalline material in a gel capsule. I don't know what the dosage was. It might have been rather low, to allow my guide to check how I would react to the medicine—or it might have been a moderate dose, but I was resisting or not recognizing its effects. In any case, after some time, when he checked in with me, I told my guide I had thought the feeling would be stronger. He could see I wasn't having any problematic reactions, and that I needed more MDMA to really experience the therapeutic journey. He then gave me a booster, which took me to a full experience.

Almost immediately, the medicine took me to my early childhood wounding. I believe reviewing the photos before the journey began likely helped. But even more, I believe my psyche was primed to receive the healing influence of the MDMA. I'm glad I had done considerable talk therapy before going on the journey.

As the notes show, I quickly went into a child state, reliving the loneliness and sense of loss I'd gone through particularly around the age of five. Transported, I stared up at the ceiling of my childhood bedroom. I could see the lamp shade, white-painted glass decorated with pictures of small, brown cowboy hats and boots, connected by a rope. There was a calmness to the vivid re-experience.

Somehow, my adult self was also present to observe and understand, also with calmness and compassion. Much healing transpired in just this first journey.

In addition to reliving these memories and gaining these insights, I also had a mystical experience. For some time, I was bathed in golden light and had no notion of self or body; I just felt a peacefulness. (See impressionistic drawing concluding this chapter.) No other forms or sounds were present. I believe this was after my childhood visitation, although my sense of time and temporal order was vague at best. It was a blessing. My understanding is that this was a gift from the Divine. A gift for my hurt psyche, a reprieve or a salve.

Commentary

The final section of my guide's notes warrants an expla-nation. During the last part of the journey, I talked about first grade (or kindergarten?), and how I cried when lining up to go home. This memory reflected my deep fear of abandonment. Although my mother did come to pick me up that day, actual abandonment as an infant, plus threats of abandonment in my early childhood, left a deep fear of abandonment within me. I remember being the only child crying that day as we lined up, believing that I wouldn't be picked up at the end of school.

The notes from my journey reflect a lonely childhood, a lot of time spent looking up at the ceiling, alone in my bedroom. They also reveal my sadness about not feeling love in my life as a child, and realizing that had hindered my development. I had no training in love. My mother was emotionally absent throughout my childhood, and my father generally was physically absent—mostly at work, and leaving child rearing to my mother.

What is not so obvious from these notes was my state of emotion, state of body, state of spirit, state of being while I was embarking on my journey. It is not like talk therapy. It's not just about words and the frontal cortex, although words and memories are part of the experience. The impact of this kind of therapeutic experience occurs deep within the body. People talk about MDMA calming the fear-holding amygdala in our brain. And maybe that is so, but this medicine's ability—in the presence of a loving guide and in a safe container—to open the heart and open the spirit, all while revisiting traumatic experiences, is absolutely special. Such a healing helper! No wonder it is slowly finding its way back to the legal landscape.

My guide was trained in a community that believed that, as a rule of thumb, therapeutic journey work should begin with two (or more) MDMA sessions before moving on to psilocybin mushrooms. This assumes the client is medically cleared for MDMA treatment. This is how my therapy began, and from my experience, the wisdom in this approach is manifest.

The MDMA deserves its moniker, the heart opener. I really felt my emotions open after just this first journey. Now, I could easily tear up—and that was not true before.

Preparation is a critical part of a successful therapeutic experience. The guide must educate the client on what to expect in general, how to prepare, and what commitment will be required for preparation and integration steps—the client's responsibility. Here, setting intentions is key. In what direction do you want to go? What do you want to work on? It's important to think about these things beforehand. However, once in the journey, it is time to let go and be with whatever wants to arise.

Responsible psychedelic use has become increasingly popular in recent years, due in no small part to the valuable contributions of author Michael Pollan and others. After speaking to several guides and understanding my own preparation, I have a few things to suggest if you are interested in pursuing psychedelic-assisted therapy.

Slow down. And make sure you have a qualified guide. A qualified guide is not likely to allow you to journey after just one or maybe even two initial meetings. They will want to get to know you and see if you are ready for this kind of work. In my case, my initial therapist, who later referred me to my guide, said to me, "Let's pump the brakes and try to learn why you are drinking." Your guide will want to assess whether your psyche is ready to stay with a potentially challenging experience, or whether you might be more likely to dissociate or resist. This is not to say such evaluations are foolproof; but it is important for a guide to actively address this question and not let a client journey if and until they are ready.

3

MDMA Journey, February 2019

Intentions

My relationship with the feminine archetype: mother to girlfriends to wives. Understand and release me from these patterns:

1. Fear of trusting and intimacy
2. Anger about unmet affection

Commune with the source. Allow love to fill and heal those hurt and neglected spaces.
Gratitude.

Setting

San Francisco Bay Area; the same journey room and guide from my first journey.

From my guide's notes

People I disappointed... I was blocked. Blocked in unhappiness.

I have to accept that I deserve to be loved, that I'm beautiful. So I can help other people.

Anger—my mother didn't want me to be whole, or couldn't. She wanted me to be like her.

My biggest fear was abandonment. I cried again and again. Terrifying cry. I cried when I was less than a year old. Nobody heard that cry.

[after landing] Write letters to brothers and prior two wives; forgiveness and gratitude.

Journey

This second MDMA journey did not require a booster. I don't know what dose I received, but presumably either it was adjusted from the last time—or I was adjusted.

In order to understand my core wounding and its significance in this journey, I must explain my history from when I was an infant. In the summer of 1952, when I was about 9 months old, my middle brother, two and a half years older than I, contracted polio. This was just a few years before a polio vaccine became available. He had a serious case, with partial paralysis. Couldn't get up off the floor. Couldn't walk. He initially went to the local hospital, but for recovery and physical therapy, he was transferred to a hospital that specialized in handling polio cases, a couple hours' drive away.

While my own memories from that time are lost, through interviews with my mother and snippets of family history I've pieced together the story: my mother decided to stay with my brother day and night for over a month. In effect, she abandoned me. I can understand her need to care for my seriously ill brother. Indeed, there was no good choice. He deserved and needed care and attention. However, in my opinion, a grave mistake was made by not trying to find some balance. Those familiar with child development will recognize that losing your primary caretaker at nine months is a terrible blow. My father continued to work, needing to support the family, and my parents hired a babysitter. My mother couldn't recall the babysitter's name, but she recollected that she had thought she was stern. My oldest brother, four and a half years older, also was at home with me.

In addition to actually abandoning me, when I was a young child my mother sometimes threatened to leave me in order to get me to "behave"—in other words, literally threatening more abandonment. I can recall one particular incident when I was three or four; my mother said she was going, and went to the hall closet, put on her winter coat, and walked out the door. She left me in hysteria. My two older brothers, bless their souls, told me she didn't mean it, but I could not recognize that. It was traumatic.

In my mother's final years of her life, our family hired a part-time hospice nurse to augment her care. She and my mother would often talk to pass the hours. A short time before my mother died at age ninety-eight, the nurse, a sweet, caring, and skillful friend, told me that my mother had confided in her that she had one big regret: she left me when I was a baby. This report was unsolicited and unexpected. The subject of abandonment was not a prior part of conversation between the nurse and me, or my mother and me. It just turned out that this life choice had haunted my mother. I told the nurse that I had forgiven my mother (this was after many more journeys). The nurse replied that she didn't believe my mother had forgiven herself.

Although so many of my journeys have been important, this particular one was a milestone in my healing process. I again traveled to a child state—actually an infant state—where I curled up into a fetal position and cried. I believe this was right after I had spoken in the adult state about how I had cried in terror and nobody came. My guide was experienced, and recognized the significance of the fetal position and the crying; he came over and cradled me in his arms and said, "I'm not leaving you." This was a huge healing moment for me, very memorable.

Commentary

Intentions often work in subtle ways. They are universally embraced as critical elements in preparing for a therapeutic journey. After this journey, I understood how my fear of trusting and intimacy—deleterious to my personal life, especially with romantic partners—connected to my being left alone to cry as a baby. I learned not to trust, to fear trusting; I gave up on trusting as a pure act of survival. This is the common origin of what psychologists term avoidant or dismissive attachment style, and a self-reliant personality/strategy/character.

Although more complete healing can take quite some time, journeys can surface so much right from the start, and great progress can be made in the early work.

My second journey also centered around my intention to understand and release my anger about unmet affection. Anger is generally generated by fear, and for me, the fear of abandonment was foundational to my sacred wound. Of course, in retrospect, like for so many of us, somewhere there is a vicious cycle. Being self-reliant and unknowingly pushing a partner away, or at least not letting them in (rejecting intimacy), and then getting angry, whether simmering or overtly, when their affection begins to dry up... Often, we talk of couples being in negative cycles, and that can be true; but the cycle can be within one individual, too. In this case: me.

Doing this work in the presence of a supportive and loving guide in a safe container is extremely important. Not that you can't do good work in a do-it-yourself way, but DIY journeys are more dangerous: a challenging journey can become a traumatizing one, and a missed opportunity. No doubt a less experienced guide would not have recognized or handled so well the healing opportunity when I went into a fetal position, especially because there was no opportunity to ask for consent before taking action by holding me. Special circumstances sometimes require exceptions. Moreover, it is well said that wounding happens in relation to a person or people (or in the absence of healthy relation, as in neglect), so it is natural that healing also happens in relation.

Integration is super important. There's a saying that integration is 80% of a journey's value, provided you are committed. The etymological root of the word "integration" is from the Latin "to make whole." In practical terms, integration means bringing the healing and growth insights and feelings into our everyday life, into our ongoing life. It means practicing daily those things that somehow relate to the journey. Otherwise, the journey will simply become a fading memory.

Unfortunately, there is a common misconception that psychedelics are a "magic pill." Perhaps the pharmaceutical industry marketed that concept into our collective brains. Well, they are not magic pills. I liken them to sacred catalysts, lubricants, door openers. Whatever your favorite descriptor is. *They* don't do the healing; *each of us* is the healer. We have the internal healer, the internal wisdom, inside of us. It's not just our birthright; it is our nature. Sometimes, we have to dig deep to let it out. These medicines can help us discover and unleash that healing power.

I don't write about integration steps in each chapter, but they were always part of the process for each journey. As you can tell from this and my prior book, I consistently practiced journaling, along with meditation and reflecting on what I had experienced and learned. Often, I went on hikes and drew. For this journey, as mentioned at the end of the notes, I wrote letters to my brothers and my two former wives. In general, letters are written soon after the journey but not actually sent until a couple of weeks after—or, indeed, not sent at all, instead placed into a "desk drawer" as perspective ripens. I did subsequently send my letters to my two former wives, acknowledging my state of mind and my limitations and their impact on our relationships.

THE HERMIT CRAB

Each house unique,
each shell unique,
each shelter hard,
each made of foreign stuff
The hermit lives alone

4

Mushroom Journey, April 2019

Intentions

Surrender and go with the journey.
Let down my defenses; be open and nonjudgmental.
Whatever needs to be healed and taught, let it please arise.
Surrender to the source. May I be released from grasping and clinging. May my heart be filled with love for all.

Setting

San Francisco Bay Area; same journey room and guide as the first journey. Eyeshades. Music.

From my guide's notes

I don't want to eat meat anymore.
My heart is getting bigger.
Letting everything go through me.
I can feel joy!
My teacher liked to chant.

Journey

As I reflect on some of these journeys, maybe all of these journeys, they look so monumental, foundation-shaking (in a good way). Shaking up the old order in my psyche to let in room for healing and growth.

This was my first magic mushroom journey in about forty-seven years! In fact, I'm pretty sure I only had one previous mushroom journey, and that was when I was twenty. And while it is totally normal even for an experienced traveler to have some trepidation before any journey, I had significant fear because of what happened back in 1972. Allow me a quick detour.

My buddy and I were touring Mexico. When we were staying in Oaxaca, we heard there were magic mushrooms in the small mountain town of San Jose del Pacifico, situated atop the Sierra Madre del Sur. That town was on the road (not a highway!) down to the Pacific coast, where we were planning to go next.

We stopped over for a night. The next morning, we walked around some dirt roads until we encountered somebody selling magic mushrooms. They looked proper, with the bluing discoloration associated with psilocybin mushrooms when bruised. We purchased some—no idea how much, but it looked like enough. We decided to take them with us to the coast, so we put them in honey to preserve them and boarded a bus with the locals and the chickens.

We made our way to Zipolite, a tiny beach area. In those days, it wasn't even a town, just a few thatched dwellings and huts. As night fell, we decided to eat the mushrooms. We had no idea how much we were eating; we were so naïve. In any case, it was too big for the both of us. After we came down, our neighbors told us that we had been rolling around on the dirt floor making lots of noises. Certainly, our psyches were overwhelmed. Two young men who got their butts kicked by the medicine spirits, you might say.

Back to the journey of April 2019. Perhaps now you can imagine the trepidation I had. Would I be rolling around on the floor again, making lots of noises? The answer to that question was no. Not that it was an "easy" journey, whatever that may be. It would be quite some time before I had anything like an easy journey at therapeutic doses. In fact, I came up with the descriptive nickname "the Celestial Washing Machine" for psilocybin mushrooms. Yes, they clean you—and they also can toss you around in so doing. I have a lot of respect for the Celestial Washing Machine.

I took a "medium" dose of three and a half grams that day, eating the dried mushrooms in a ceremonial style by biting off little pieces with my front teeth. That method is intended to remind the participant that they are taking a sacrament, not a food. I rolled the little bits around in my mouth for some time, getting them nice and soggy before swallowing them and taking in the next little bit. Consequently, eating these mushrooms took at least fifteen minutes.

One word about my dose. It doesn't take a Ph.D. in chemistry, which I have, to be aware that not all mushrooms have the same concentration of active ingredients. It appears that most people who use these materials don't seem to care. They just weigh them and assume they are all the same. With gadflies like me making noise, that is slowly changing; and because labs are reporting a wide range in concentration, even more testing is happening.

My guide, as was his custom, left me alone to consume the medicine. I was going so slowly that I believe I was just finishing eating the mushrooms when he returned. I slid under the sheet and blanket and put on my eye mask, and the journey began.

One of the first things I recall was suddenly sitting up, eye mask still on, and saying, "I don't want to eat meat anymore." I have no idea where that came from. I wasn't reflecting on animals at all, as far as I can recall. The pronouncement just seemed to come out of nowhere. But to this day, I no longer eat meat. The idea seems repulsive to me. I know the environmental and moral reasoning against eating meat, but somehow my decision seemed to come from somewhere else, perhaps from some new, deeper awareness of sentient beings.

(I have had stress about this vegetarian choice, and I eat seafood as a compromise at family dinners, a choice I continue to make and continue to question as of this writing.)

While I said "my heart is getting bigger," I repeatedly moved my arms and hands over my heart, spreading them wide and then back in again in an "open, open, open" motion. There was love coursing through me. Kind of like blowing a kiss from my heart instead of my lips.

Further on in the journey, I said, "Letting everything go through me." I believe this referred to taking in the suffering of people and the world. This is a bodhisattva effort: accepting others' suffering in order to relieve it, yet doing so without holding it or being contaminated by it.

The Celestial Washing Machine was cleaning me and teaching me. What more could there be? It was awesome!

But there was indeed more. I was overcome with the most incredible sense of joy I have ever felt. I exclaimed, "I can feel joy!" It had to be divine joy. Like all of us, I've had moments of great happiness and joy in my life: when my two children were born, and during other terrific events—a big career success, wonderful love making, my team winning the World Series, and so on. But this felt different, both in intensity and in that it seemed to come out of "nowhere," which I take to be from Spirit. Especially for someone like myself, who has suffered from lifelong mild depression (dysthymia) where joy is a rare commodity, this was like a kiss from heaven. Fair to say that this celestial kiss didn't last, but it sure gave me a taste of the nectar of divine joy, truly a gift.

The music varies with each journey, and the music for mushroom journeys has a different character than MDMA music. At some point, my guide changed the music to Tibetan chanting, featuring that low, deep voice. This connected me to my first Zen teacher, the late Seung Sahn, who was a great believer in chanting and a wonderful chanter himself. I said, "My teacher liked to chant." I then thought about my other Zen teachers. I realized I carried considerable tension about them. There was a history of attraction, respect, a desire to know what they knew (or what I believed they knew). But there also was an aversion associated with distrust, hence the tension.

I told my guide, with respect to his own training, "You must have had good guides." As soon as those words left my lips, I burst into a torrent of crying, uncontrollable crying. My guide stroked the hair on my head, comforting me, and within just twenty or so seconds, this big crying spell stopped. What was that about? What prompted it? Where did it come from? I had no idea.

It wasn't until the next day that I realized there was only one other time in my adult life when I cried like that. It was the very moment, thirty-some years ago, when I dropped dirt onto my father's casket. And suddenly, all became clear—the Celestial Washing Machine's teaching and healing. (See the drawing at the conclusion of this chapter made as part of integration.)

Up until then, my father had played only a minor role in the work of healing my childhood trauma; I had largely focused on my mother in my therapy. But the father is an archetype, an authority figure, protector, and teacher; and now, in this journey, my father's importance was revealing itself. I reflected on the truth that my father had largely been absent during my child-hood, and this absence of a loving and wise father was another part of my developmental trauma.

The teaching? First, I learned that I have had deep-seated psychological confusion stemming from wanting a present, loving father and teacher. Because I did not receive this from my biological father, I have been attracted to Zen teachers as substitutes. However, this attraction has come with distrust, based both on my experience of not being able to count on my father and on the perceptible limitations of these teachers.

This realization has also helped clarify that learning is up to me. I must trust myself. As Buddha reportedly said on his death bed, "Be a light unto yourself." I take this lesson to heart and have given up my interest in Zen priests, although I respect when clergy of any religion, including indigenous traditions, perform their roles well.

The healing? I have finally buried my father. The emotional outburst and learning and healing that followed gave me deep closure.

I'm capable, myself. I am light. I have internal wisdom. Just like all of us.

What an incredible journey in the Celestial Washing Machine! The places this medicine took me; the lessons, the joy, the healing it provided!

Commentary

Quite an amazing journey, so full of big events and lessons. Not every journey is chock full of these consequential moments and insights, but this one sure was. So different from my mushroom journey in Mexico as a young man by the Pacific Ocean.

This journey day, I became a vegetarian, at least mostly.

I experienced divine joy, really felt touched by the divine in a profound and loving way. How big is that?! Some might expect divine joy from an MDMA journey and not so much from psilocybin mushrooms, but obviously they would be mistaken. Both medicines deliver.

I experienced closure around my father and his death. Associated with that was insight into a decades-long tension and confusion around Zen priests. This turn in the journey could be attributed to the choice and timing of the Tibetan chanting music, and illustrates how important the music can be.

5

The Intrinsic Duality of Nature and the Opportunity Principle

The wave vs. particle duality is a fundamental and famous aspect of the theory of quantum physics. This is not the place for any detailed explanation of quantum physics, but let me say just a bit more. First, there's another "uncertainty" in our understanding of quantum phenomena, and it is aptly called the Uncertainty Principle—also famous. The uncertainty principle states that there is an intrinsic uncertainty in knowing with precision both a particle's momentum and its position, or its energy and time. That is, if you determine one of the two variables precisely, then the other of the two becomes wildly uncertain. You can't know both precisely. The uncertainty principle by itself says a lot about our world, right? We're uncertain about just about everything!

So back to the wave-particle duality: it turns out that depending on the type of observation (the measurement), "things" (i.e. matter) like electrons and photons manifest as wave or particle phenomena—but not simultaneously as both. I want to add one more piece. Not so famous, but also part of the basic theoretical development of quantum physics, is the fact that it can be shown that the uncertainty principle makes it impossible to simultaneously observe properties of matter as a wave and as a particle. Only one or the other is possible.

I just find this fascinating. And it makes me think about another intrinsic duality, and that is spirit and flesh. Or, if you will, spirit and matter, or spirit and material beings or objects. I like to say spirit and flesh, since we're made of flesh. Now here's the question. Is it impossible to simultaneously observe both aspects? Well, I'm uncertain about that! However, I am certain that both exist, and that's important.

The materialists believe there is only flesh. I beg to differ, based on my experiences. Alas, I can't prove there is spirit, too, but I invite everyone to explore. Most importantly for me is my belief—my faith—that spirit and flesh are one and the same, indistinguishable.

There is yet one more duality that deserves recognition and reflection. This comes from the Buddhist world view: form and emptiness. The well-known Heart Sutra includes the line, "Form is emptiness and emptiness form." The sutra says they are one and the same.

We are familiar with form. Form is matter—objects, birds, people, trees, mountains, whales, oceans, planets, galaxies. But what is emptiness?

Is emptiness the same as spirit? This is a tantalizing question. Since no one is likely to prove me wrong here on this plane of existence, I feel free to offer my opinion. And that is, *Yes*. "Emptiness" and "spirit" are two names for the same thing. I suspect there are different planes or manifestations of spirit, emptiness. Just like there are different manifestations of matter. Something to investigate!

And yet, there is still another conundrum. It can be argued that the greatest delusion people suffer from is that they are solely their body. Some say that we are soul or spirit temporarily clothed by our body. If spirit and flesh are one, does that contradict the idea that we are not our bodies? I myself believe we are not solely or even primarily our bodies, although they are our temporary home. This points to a more subtle, perhaps complex relationship between flesh and spirit, form and emptiness. The Great Mystery!

Here's a final word on the subject of the intrinsic duality of nature. If waves and particles are different manifestations of the same matter, and form is emptiness and flesh is spirit, then wouldn't it be better to speak of the intrinsic *unity* of nature, instead of an intrinsic duality?

Well, if you are ready for one more idea after this talk of duality, unity, and the Great Mystery, here is another way to look at the Uncertainly Principle. Seems to me that this principle is always expressed with some negative slant. *You can't...* Like some finger wagging. Is there a positive viewpoint? Starting with the physics: if you know one of those two aspects precisely, then the other is *free* to be anything! And this freedom represents an opportunity—hence the Opportunity Principle. Or I suppose, the Freedom Principle could be its name too.

My intuition tells me the Opportunity Principle is fundamental to our lives. It's about freedom of choice, free will, agency. It represents the opportunity to grow in love and spiritual maturity, and heal old wounds. Isn't that why we are here on Earth? Oh yeah, and to play in the Garden. As such, the Opportunity Principle is at the heart of the Great Mystery.

THE MYSTERY

The mystery winks at us
and invites us to come closer.
Beyond all form,
using each of our senses,
staying curious,
following the scent
of sublime wisdom.
Hear the crackle of the fire,
see the flames dance,
warming the heart

6

Mushroom Journey, May 2019

Intentions

Surrender and go with the journey.
Whatever needs to be healed, let it please arise.
Please teach me. May I be a channel of your love and joy.

Setting

San Francisco Bay Area; the same room and guide as for the first three journeys. The recorded music was new; it was different for each journey.

From my guide's notes

I surrender— please love me.
It's okay to ask for love. I need it, too. A lot of people love me.
I dance for people, for their pain, so I can be a part of their tribe.
Taking a lot of pain.

Taking the pain—it's so beautiful.

Coming to peace with feeling other people's suffering.

To be a bodhisattva, you have to take other people's problems.

Journey into pain, bodhisattva path.

Journey

This time, we raised the dosage to four and a half grams of dried mushrooms. My intentions for my second psilocybin mushroom journey were rather open-ended, as you can tell.

As my guide and I sat in front of the altar before our ceremony, he asked me if there was anything else I wanted to work on, perhaps something more specific. "Yes," I said. I told him I was feeling some self-doubt; not so much mentally, but in my body. Self-doubt, doubt about others, doubt about God, doubt about any and everything—this is a characteristic effect of childhood trauma. He said he thought that some body and energy work would be helpful.

The journey began with me chanting a mantra over and over: "I surrender. Please love me." I felt the acceptance coming from being loved, and some deeper understanding and body-feeling, a relaxation, that I am lovable.

However, it didn't take long for the journey to take an unexpected turn. And it was the music my guide was playing that was the catalyst.

A female vocalist was singing a song, not in English. I'm not sure it was in any language, actually. But at least in my psychic state it sounded plaintive, evocative of suffering, pain. It sounded like the singer was voicing a great lost love. For most of this experience, this was a journey into pain.

At one point, following what we had discussed at the outset, my guide performed some body work on me. With very little pressure on my quadriceps, I shouted, "PAIN!!" Pain stored deep in my body was let loose. How much remained? I don't know, but after the journey I felt significant relief.

The melodies kept coming. There was a stretch of highly energetic music, excellent music to dance to, and, lying on my back with eyeshades on, that is what I did. I moved my hands and arms in rhythm, really getting into the energy of the music. I said, "I dance for people, for their pain, so I can be part of their tribe. Taking a lot of pain. Taking the pain. It's so beautiful." Soon after, I said, "Coming to peace with feeling other people's suffering." And some time after that, I said, "To be a bodhisattva, you have to be with other people's problems. Sometimes, there's nothing you can do for their pain; just be with them." The last sentence made me cry in grief for the great suffering in the world I could feel.

You don't normally associate peace, freedom, or even beauty with pain, with being open to others' pain. But being open, vulnerable is what makes us whole, connected; and that leads to peace and the beauty of wholeness and compassion. Not running away from, fearing, avoiding, or walling ourselves off from other people's pain, or our own pain, as I so often did in the past.

I believe the Divine is helping me to sit with pain, and helping me to help others to sit with their pain, as well. It's providing me with the celestial energy to dance for their pain, connecting me to the tribe and the tribe to me. I hope this makes sense. I hope you can connect with this dance.

Commentary

Love and pain. Peace and beauty when feeling into, grieving for universal suffering. That's what this journey was about. Let's say it was an opportunity to walk the bodhisattva path, to feel into that path. Perhaps surprisingly, there was dancing energy associated with this pain. Lifeforce! To be alive is to suffer and experience love and compassion. They are inseparable. How can there be compassion without suffering?

This experience also reminds me of tonglen, which is an especially popular practice in Tibetan Buddhism. In brief, it is a meditation practice of taking in pain and suffering around you and transforming them into and releasing relief, love, and peace.

Noteworthy also was the connection to tribe. Tribe is connection, belonging with other people. Knowing that we are a part of something bigger, community.

DARKNESS AND LIGHT

Famous words, Let there be Light!
How would we know light without darkness?
Accepting light, we accept darkness.
Rooted in darkness,
rooted in mud,
from the earth
we take human form

We fear separation, loss, pain, destruction,
because we experience separation, loss, pain and
        destruction.
Don't forget pestilence, war, tsunamis, wild fires

Why are we here?
Survival of the fittest?
Dragging ourselves out of the sea,
watching for danger,
always on the move,
searching for food, procreation,
and don't forget love, too

Famous words, Let your love light shine!
Give yourself to love! Love is all there is!
Remember and enjoy the
hope, gratitude, compassion, forgiveness,

wild acts of kindness,

kisses and caresses,

hugs and honey,

mother's milk and mangos,

morning star and vibrant sunsets

Samsara and nirvana—same or different?

If you say same, you're wrong.

If you say different, you're wrong.

What to do?

7

Group Mushroom Journey in the Woods, July 2019

Intentions

Surrender and go with the journey.
Trust in God's love.
Trust that I am part of nature.
Trust that I belong with people.

Setting

Secluded redwood forest in the San Francisco Bay Area.

Notes taken by me after the Journey

Please make me a channel of your love. Answer: then you have to die.
No fear.
Everything is God.
Humble yourself to the medicine.

Journey

This was a group experience. It was small as groups go, with just five journeyers, three women and two men. Four of us were over fifty years old; three of us were over sixty. Our male guide had a female assistant. We met in a small clearing, perhaps ten meters across, in a secluded redwood forest. The larger trees were very tall, stately giants, and smaller ones were mixed in, too. Although probably not old growth trees, these trees were still rising to two hundred feet (sixty meters). We arranged our sleeping bags in a circle, with a Mexican blanket as an altar on the circle's perimeter. There was space on both sides of the altar for the two guides to sit.

Our guide placed various objects on the altar: two Virgin Guadalupe candles and a few Mexican shamanic objects, including a rattle, a feathered piece, part of the antlers from a small deer, a braid made of reeds, a beaded necklace, and smudging sage in an abalone shell.

Each of the journeyers were invited to place a power object of their own onto the altar. I brought a small Buddha carved from green stone, and a dense black rock from a beach in Santorini. The Buddha was holding a small pagoda, which houses sacred relics. The volcanic rock, smoothed by the crashing waves of the Aegean Sea, represented the earth and its great transformations. Other participants brought crystals, shells, and a bust of the Buddha.

There were no tents. No toilets; just a small dug-out latrine. Rustic.

We arrived about noon on a pleasant summer day. There were activities during the daytime and the journey began just before sunset. We journeyed and slept in our sleeping bags. We wore eyeshades for the inward journey. There was no recorded music, just the sounds of nature, including the sounds of some of the journeyers.

My dose was five grams of dried mushrooms. This was my first group experience, and my third experience in the Celestial Washing Machine.

I noticed the two guides had taken off their shoes and socks and were walking barefoot on the forest floor after we arrived at our camp. I decided to join them, to feel the earth—mostly matted redwood needles—beneath my feet.

None of us had ever journeyed together, and we didn't know each other well at all. So, for our first community activity, each of us spoke for roughly ten minutes about why we were there and what our intentions were. Often, intentions are about what you want to heal or develop or understand: Where do I want to go? What do I hope to get out of the journey?

People told brief stories about the pain in their lives and the symptoms that manifested for them. Several of us mentioned the terribleness in our childhoods. Most of us were quite revealing during this exercise, and it surely was the best thing we could have done to get to know each other and to understand with compassion the road each of us had walked. This truthfulness and vulnerability brought us together as a group.

I decided to begin with my intentions and then give my background. Along with the intentions I wrote before arriving at the ceremony (outlined above), I added: "To grow as a bodhi-sattva." Although I thought everyone in the group, including the non-Buddhists, would understand what that meant, the leader asked me to define the term. I explained that a bodhisattva is someone dedicated to helping others—as a situation arises, as a situation calls for. I said that although my dreams reveal that I still need more healing, I believe I've done much of my healing from childhood trauma and that I have undergone a real trans-formation. (It turns out that although I *had* made great progress, there was still plenty to heal!) I told the group that since taking my second and most recent mushroom journey, I've felt that my energy now could be directed mostly toward helping others.

After this short discussion of my intentions, I mentioned the trauma I had experienced during my early childhood, and commented on how common developmental trauma was—probably everyone in the group had suffered so. I described how I had used cannabis and alcohol to manage my pain, and that quitting alcohol (generally a bottle of wine at night) was what brought me into psychotherapy. I also explained how my striving for success (resulting in a Ph.D. and an accomplished career) represented a typical strategy to win the love I didn't receive as a child. (Another person in our group told a similar tale of needing to over-achieve.)

It was not difficult to open up and be honest in the community setting. There was a sense of safety and acceptance, of honoring each other, and that helped us bond. But we weren't finished with this preparation yet.

Our next activity was to build a nature altar. This exercise, meant to connect us with our environment, took about one hour and was performed in silence. The leader chose a tree and we constructed the altar in front of it and on its bark. We gathered pieces from the forest floor around us and together we placed them on the altar, creating and decorating designs, working from each other's contributions. There were sticks and leaves of all sorts, pieces of moss, bark, redwood cones. We ended up with a beautiful woven tapestry of natural elements.

The next exercise continued our bonding and was performed to music. We paired up and stood still, only a foot or so distance between our bodies, and gazed into each other's eyes while our guide sang these and similar lyrics, at times repeating them:

Here is a neighbor just like you who wants
to be happy
Just like you, just like me
Here is a neighbor just like you who is a
broken child
Just like you, just like me
Here is a neighbor just like you who longs for joy
Just like you, just like me

Here is a neighbor just like you who wants
to be loved
Just like you, just like me

After a few minutes, we switched partners, repeating the exercise until everyone had a turn with each person. This special bonding experience helped us open our hearts to each other.

By now, it was mid-afternoon. We were still hours before beginning the journey itself; the ingestion of the earth medicine was planned for shortly before sundown, and the summer day was long. Our guide told us we would spend the rest of the afternoon alone, to go a little way into the redwoods and mindfully create a Deathbed from the forest material. Then we were instructed to lie down in that bed and prepare for death. Our leader would ring a bell when it was time to return to our camp, in about three hours.

There were several trails in the area, and I followed one for a ten-minute barefoot walk. When you are looking for a place to die, you select it mindfully, carefully. Not just any place will do for such an important event. I scouted as I walked down the narrow path, until I came across a small, picturesque clearing. The left side of the path was pretty with moss and ferns, but there was a slope to the ground and I wanted a flat death bed. On the other side of the path, there was a little open area, thick with redwood needles and flanked by lush ferns. I sensed this would be a good place to die.

I took my time feeling the environment around me. I decided a simple bed "frame" was all I needed. I constructed a rectangular border from the available forest material. On the two long sides, I used twigs and small branches shed from the redwoods. I used some bark for the head and foot of the border, decorated with small redwood cones, about a half-inch across. I cleared the area within the border, removing forest debris and leaving only the soft redwood needles.

Then, I sat down on my creation, resting and getting a feel for the bed and the surroundings. I spent considerable time looking at the trees—their beauty, and how the dappled sunlight brought out the colors of the red bark and the green branches. I heard a few birds singing.

When I was ready, I lay down. I took in the forest around me from this new perspective, looking directly up at the tall redwoods. After more time passed, I was ready to begin my good-byes.

I began with my two children. I spoke to them in my mind, telling them how much I loved them and that I hoped they would live long lives with much happiness. I said I was sorry for the mistakes that I had made, but that overall, I was content with all the love I had given them. I accepted that my life would slowly fade from their memories.

Then, I said farewell to my brothers. They kept me sane in childhood, although as the youngest, I was sometimes the object of their frustration and pain. I thanked them for our secure bond and wished them some of the healing that I have experienced. I wished them peace and happiness.

My friends came last, and there were quite a few. I called out to each of my close friends one by one, hoping I wasn't forgetting any. I told them how important they were to me and how I loved them. I thanked them for our sharing and learning together, for just being together, accepting each other, making life more complete.

Then I lay quietly, looking up into the trees. I noticed the sun was getting lower and most of the light was blocked by the forest. I started to feel a chill. The temperature was dropping quickly now, as we were getting closer to sunset. I felt both satisfaction and sadness about my goodbyes. I felt ready to let go and let the earth take me back.

A distant bell called. Closer, it rang. I sat up and turned to look behind me. Our leader was walking toward me, coming to bring me back to the group, to the unknown journey into life and death that awaited that night, to a place I couldn't anticipate, couldn't predict. A journey of healing and insight, I hoped. I sensed it would be a difficult journey.

The group gathered and the leader explained how we would proceed. We each would come up to the side of the altar where he was sitting and receive our medicine. The assistant guide sat on the other side of the altar, watching closely. About an hour after we began eating, our leader would ring a bell signifying the start of the group journey; and he would ring the bell again at the end of the journey, roughly six hours after that, or whenever he felt the time was right.

We came up one by one and kneeled before our guide to receive our medicine. He had a small, portable electronic scale in front of him, and a bag of beautiful, intact dried psilocybin mushrooms. He asked each of us what weight of mushrooms we wanted. He and I had talked about this beforehand; I imagined each of us had done so. But of course, as the moment came, we could change our minds. The magnitude of the dose is of consequence. We had discussed five grams for me, and I stayed with that number.

We each sat with our legs inside our sleeping bags. It was now quite chilly, and the day's heat was leaving through the clear, blue sky above us. Sunset was close and the light dimming. We held our mushrooms on our laps, slowly ingesting our medicine in the traditional Mazatec manner, chewing with our front teeth, holding the mushroom bits in our mouth until well wet before swallowing. The assistant guide came around periodically with a jar of honey that we could dip our finger into and add a little sweetness.

It takes some time to eat five dried grams in this way, but it was not difficult or unpleasant for me. This was a sacred partaking of the earth's medicine. A blessing and an honor to be given the opportunity, to be accepted as part of the group. It was a ceremony in nature intended to affirm our awe of the mystery of life.

As evening descended, the only light came from two Virgin Guadalupe candles. After eating, we laid down in our sleeping bags and put on our eyeshades. Although we were in our circle and could hear each other, this was going to be a solo trip for each of us.

It doesn't take long to begin to feel the effects when you eat the mushrooms like this. The journey was clearly beginning, punctuated by a few yawns, a common symptom of ascending. I knew I was already setting out on the journey when I heard the bell marking the official start for the group.

Here are the highlights of the journey that I recall.

At the outset, I really did feel like I was being tossed around by the agitator of the Celestial Washing Machine. I don't know what my body was doing, but I was feeling as though I was being twisted this way and that. I know I was being cleaned by the medicine. It wasn't comfortable, but I was okay with it. Our leader came by, knelt by my side and whispered in my ear, "How are you doing?" I told him, "I'm well. I'm cleaning" (meaning, I was being cleaned). He patted me, and, seeing that I was fine, went to check on the next person.

When you're on the journey, the concept of time generally disappears—but I know I was in the Celestial Washing Machine's agitator for quite a while. What exactly was being cleaned, I couldn't say, but I know that was what was happening. The medicine was cleaning me and healing me.

Then, there was a shift. A calmness came over me. I felt myself drifting upward to the stars, to the heavens. I came back to my intentions, but instead of "May I grow as a bodhisattva," I began saying to myself, "Please make me a channel of your love, make me a channel of your love." Then, I was in the presence of the Great Spirit. It wasn't a man with a white beard, but a sort of mystical understanding, ineffable. I said again, "Make me a channel of your love." An answer came back: "Then you have to die." And with that, I dissolved into the heavens. I was no more.

There were stars. There was beauty. There was the divine. There was love.

I believe most of the journey was up in the stars, which were literally above us in the clear night. Eventually, I felt that I was coming back into a body, reassembling a bit at a time. I remember not really caring if I was going to be in a body again.

I remember my neighbor making some noise, having a challenging journey. (It turned out well for her.) The thought arose: *I wonder if she's dying.* Then another thought arose: *Maybe I'm dying, too.* If so, it didn't seem to matter. There was no fear.

Around this time, the leader came over and did some body work on me, which felt great. I was totally pliant. He also did energy work, probing and feeling the energy flowing through my body.

Soon after, I began coming down. I felt peaceful. Our guide sang for us. Here are some partial lyrics of three of the songs that I remember:

The whole world is a very narrow bridge
And the most important thing
Is to have no fear at all

                        — Rabbi Nachman of Breslov

La ilaha illa Allah
Everything is God and God is everything

                        — Muslim prayer, loosely translated

Humble yourself in front of the medicine
You gotta bend down low
Humble yourself in front of the medicine
Ask it what it knows.

We shall lift each other up
higher and higher
We shall lift each other up.

                        — Rainbow hippie song

Then the bell rang, signifying the end of the journey. The most intense part was over. Six or so hours had passed since the first bell. Before we began the journey, our leader had asked if anyone wanted to sing when we were done. I had raised my hand, thinking it would be some sort of sing-along. Instead, he said to me, "Sit up and sing." I had no idea what to sing. Obviously unprepared, no song was in my head. I heard my fellow journeyers, and I said, "I hear your beautiful voices." And there was some laughing, some happy, warm feelings. Then someone said, "I love you, Chris." I said, "Thank you." Then I sang "Beautiful Love." I believe I actually created a melody, singing, "Beautiful, beautiful love." Those were the only two words. The song probably lasted a minute. Funny, thinking about it now. Sweet, too.

Next, our two guides placed snacks in the middle of our circle, the two candles providing all our light. All vegetarian food, of course. Mostly fruits and nuts. We needed some nourishment after the long and strenuous journey we all had experienced, and we hadn't eaten since before 10 AM. It was now probably 2 AM. There was some talking as we gathered closer, eating, sharing. Clearly, there was a wonderful, loving feeling between all of us journeyers.

Next was sleep. We settled back in our bags to get some well-earned rest.

In the morning, we gathered in a tight circle. The guides brought out more food, and we shared and ate well. The food tasted delicious.

After we all helped clean up, we sat in a circle a little way away from our camp. It was time to share our journey experiences. One by one, the five of us reported, taking about ten minutes each. After each person spoke, each of the other journeyers would respond with something supportive and loving, sometimes with just a simple "I love your smile," or "You were so brave." Then, the guides would say something supportive and perhaps give a little guidance. I sensed I should go last. It just seemed appropriate.

After I reported on my mystical experience, the leader said that I showed the warrior spirit, seeking the divine. He also said that when he checked my body energy, the energy was freely flowing through me. Perhaps I was like a channel. This journey anchored my understanding that I am to serve, to tread the path of a bodhisattva.

After our sharing, we packed up our camp and hiked back to our cars, where we hugged and said our good-byes.

Integration work with the leader subsequently followed, as is customary and needed after every journey. Writing is also part of the integration process for me.

Commentary

Group journeys for healing and spiritual growth are an integral part of the traditions of indigenous peoples in North and South America and Africa. In the newer and still developing Western practice of healing with psychedelics (entheogens), the group experience also has taken root. This adds the aspect of community that is missing in an individual journey. And when the experience takes place outside in a peaceful natural setting, it also adds the aspect of environment or nature.

Why does this kind of psychedelic medicine work in groups? We are social animals; we are psychologically designed to be within community. Group energy is uplifting in inspirational and ritualistic occasions. This same effect occurs in meditation groups, drum circles, dance troupes—they produce a collective energy, encouraging participants to stay on the path.

Journeying in a group brings a natural connection to humanity. Every individual is at a different stage of development and has different needs, and yet everyone is a truly valued member. Realizing this provides a warm, welcoming feeling, a feeling of safety. You aren't the only person in need of healing or spiritual growth. It's also humbling: to know that in the journey ahead, you might be the one calling out for help, showing your vulnerability. These are all healthy, wonderful reasons to journey in a group—assuming the people in the group are well chosen and the group is under the care of a skilled and experienced guide-therapist. This certainly was the case in the redwood forest.

All in all, I am so thankful for our guides, my fellow journeyers, the earth medicine, the wonderful mystical experience, and the love I bathed in and feel now.

This journey into the Celestial Washing Machine was all the more rewarding because of the lasting community we formed. And the environment of the grand redwood forest—with earth below us, sky above us—formed a nurturing container where life and death could both dissolve and healing and spiritual growth could emerge.

There is an intriguing connection between the afternoon exercise of creating and lying in a deathbed in the redwood forest, and my dying during the nighttime journey. What kind of connection is it? Is this better called synchronicity, or priming the pump? However I look at it, it's staring back at me. Without question, there is value and opportunity in well-crafted activities accompanying with journeying, like the deathbed experience and the bonding activities with others in the group.

My experience of dying during the journey is an example of ego dissolution, or "ego death," a non-dual experience, and merging with the divine. Current psychedelic discussions and literature touch a lot on ego death; in my opinion, some of it is helpful and some unhelpful. I have written down my perspectives on the topic in the next chapter.

After this journey, I wrote a poem titled "Bed in the Woods." It's included in my prior book. Subsequently, two friends and I were talking about poetry and one of them suggested we create a kintsugi poem. She picked that name—kintsugi—because it references the Japanese art form where broken pottery is reassembled using gold or silver glue, creating a new beautiful object. So the three of us each contributed a poem, mine being "Bed in the Woods," and we broke them into pieces and reassembled them into a new poem, with a little glue. Here it is.

ADIEU, A KINTSUGI POEM

Sunlight kisses my face
as I look up at the tall Redwood trees.
I lay among the glowing green ferns and red bark
on a soft bed of matted needles.
There is a narrow path to one side
on which my family, my friends slowly approach.
I am not sure if it is hello or goodbye?
When they arrive, I offer them each a twig or branch
of love, of gratitude.
Tears are healing, I say

Last night, I dreamt about a wound that
        would not heal.
I peered into the ring of fiery flesh.
Leaning forward I tumbled in.
I fell deep into the wound, then out the other side,
flying past the Moon, planets, and galaxies of stars
in a free fall through vast oceans of darkness
until suddenly Death appeared

Death was not the snarling wolf I had feared,
ready to tear my flesh from bone.
No, Death was a big fat bear in a tie-dyed t-shirt
standing in a field of tall grass wild with
        yellow daisies

He looked up smiling,
the sunlight kissing his face.
Wrapping his big furry arms around me,
he pointed to a door.
Laughing he said,
"Before I bid you Adieu,
know that there is Nothing ....
Nothing ever to fear"

Here in the forest,
a door on the giant redwood tree swings open.
A warm west wind carries me forward.
I marvel at the door frame—
a masterpiece of carved wood depicting saints
hugging smiling demons and curious animals I have
            never seen

I drift down a long hallway
with frescos of my ancestors—
Hunters, gatherers, peasants farming fields, artisans,
warriors...the oppressed and the oppressors

Next the scenes of my own life appear like
            holograms.
And as my body dies, I see my grown children
holding the twigs and branches I gave them
as they cry their healing tears

Drifting further, I see my children living out
    their lives
until they are old, gray-haired, wise and
lying on beds of matted needles in the
    redwood forest,
their children and grandchildren surrounding them.
As the Sunlight kisses them Adieu,
I smile as I realize… I am all of them

by Finlay "Goldie" Boag, Karin Denevi, and
Chris Becker

8

Ego Death

Psychedelics are now widely discussed in mainstream media, as well as in countless lesser-known spaces. One aspect of this broad topic that frequently comes up is ego death, or ego dissolution.

What is ego death? As the phrase suggests, it means losing any notion of self during a journey. A good alternative word is non-dual. Beyond that, there is room for different reported experiences and commentary. Ego death often is implicitly understood to be, and even explicitly identified as being an important goal of journeying. I've talked with individuals who took medicine like magic mushrooms and worried when they didn't experience ego death; they felt like something was wrong with them. Such unmet expectations about ego death can reinforce common core beliefs stemming from childhood wounding—obviously not a good thing. I've also heard and read plenty of boasting about ego death experiences; this "macho medicine" is immature and equally unhelpful.

Consequently, the first thing I'd like to advise about ego death is… don't worry about it. If you haven't experienced it yet, maybe you will later. If you don't end up experiencing it in this lifetime, that's still okay. I suggest not making it a goal.

It is also common to feel fearful in anticipation of ego death. Fear can arise when the ego (sense of self) believes it is being threatened with extinction. Sometime this fear can be overpowering, and can even block the approaching transition. I would like to offer an alternative perspective that may help: Once you've crossed over to an ego death experience, there is no fear at all—because there is no longer any sense of self that can feel threatened. There is just the experience, often one of wisdom and bliss. Keeping this in mind may alleviate worry about ego extinction, although of course this is easier said than done.

It is also true that our memory of the experience can sometimes be weak, or even absent. This shouldn't be surprising, given the nature of ego death. Although sometimes we can recall all sorts of details—spirits, ancestors, realms, and so on—we're often just left with a vague impression of merging into Divine Light. This might be frustrating; the ego does really like memory! But even if recall is elusive, do not discount the significance of the experience. Memory is not always an indicator of the gathering of spiritual wisdom or the process of healing.

What about integration? How to bring it home? Regardless of how intensely (or not) you've experienced the non-dual, I encourage intentional reflection with gratitude. And if detailed memory is available, there are many rituals that can enhance those memories and bring them into daily life. Journaling, singing, chanting, drawing, dancing, specific meditations, and a thousand other practices... creativity is welcome.

Wishing you beautiful, fulfilling journeys, with or without ego death.

DANCE

In the flow,
like water through streams,
wind through trees,
blood through veins,
air through nostrils,
thoughts through mind,
feelings through body,
body through space.
Energy flows
in a dance of love,
dance of life.
Red leaves dance before the bright blue sky

9

Mushroom Journey, August 2019

Intentions

Please continue to purify, heal, and teach me, so I may grow as a bodhisattva.

May I be a channel of your love.

Thanks be to God!

Setting

San Francisco Bay Area, morning; back in the same journey room as before, a solo journey and with the same trusted guide. Recorded music.

From my guide's notes

I have to slow down and ask for things.

Cleaning, letting go of my attachment to the world. It needs me to let go. It's waiting for me to let go…

I have to ask for help, God's help, to understand.

Ask for breath, help me breathe.

White light, purifying. Divine discussion—do I come back?
Can see Dogen was not fully purified. Can't fool me.
Family trauma, murder, Nazis.

Journey

Journeys are so unpredictable, taking you where you need
to go—at least that's the general belief, which I don't quarrel
with. Sometimes there are vistas of wonderfully uplifting and
exquisite fields, and sometimes deep, dark recesses and pain.
This journey was no different, featuring both these extremes.

I was exploring a range of effective doses, and chose to
increase it to six grams of dried mushrooms for this journey.

My intentions were open-ended. I wrote them on paper
and placed them on the altar.

As we sat together in front of the altar, my guide uttered
a beautiful prayer, which concluded with the following: "May
Chris learn as much as he is ready to learn, heal as much as he
is ready to heal, grow as much as he is ready to grow." These
words turned out to ring true.

I ate the dried mushrooms in the traditional Mazatec way,
biting and chewing with only my front teeth, holding the wet
bits in my mouth, often under my tongue. I occasionally used a
little honey, but the taste of the earth medicine is okay for me.
It takes some time to eat six grams in this way, perhaps twenty
or thirty minutes. Toward the end of the eating, I could feel the

strength of the medicine coming on. I ate the last few bits more quickly, and then lay down wearing my eyeshades.

According to my guide's notes, as I was ascending I talked about "asking." I said I had to slow down and make sure I ask people for permission. In reflection, this included a desire to be more willing to be vulnerable, this asking. I subsequently said that I was "cleaning, letting go of my attachment to the world…" This is surely a process. And letting go of attachment to the world does not mean not being engaged, but rather not grasping. I then said, "I have to ask for help, God's help, help me understand, ask for breath, help me breathe." This reflected a surrendering feeling, a call for myself to let go and know that I can call on the Divine.

As I continued to ascend and reach the height of the medicine's power, my guide said I lay still for a couple hours. I don't remember much in the way of events or thinking from this period of time, except that I know that much of it was spent in white light, with no sense of self. I believe I was being purified, or so it felt.

At some point, there was a Divine conversation about whether I should come back. I was probably beginning my slow descent from the height of the medicine's effect, and my ego was re-forming. At first, it wasn't clear that I should or could return. The conversation involved me saying that some people need me. This went on for a while, until I realized I was in my body again.

At this point, I wanted to take off my eyeshades, and I said I was coming down. It was apparent, however, that I was still journeying. My guide mentioned later that I journeyed for a good while with my eyes open, unusual for this setting.

With my consent, my guide performed some body work on me, including stretching me over his back while I was standing up. This work felt good and I was relaxed, but I was low on energy, so we took a break and I ate a little honey and some grapes to increase my blood sugar.

Relaxing but still actively journeying without my eyeshades, I began speaking about a Zen talk I had given recently. I began by saying, "Who would have thought that the *Dhammapada* is wrong?" Originating from the Pali Canon, the *Dhammapada* is a foundational piece for all of Buddhism. I remember saying, "I'm not trying to invent anything, just set the record straight"—referencing my belief that Gautama Buddha didn't say some of the things he was reported to have said. I found the whole notion so fundamentally bizarre that it actually seemed extremely funny, and my guide later commented that I was often giggling during this part of my journey.

I told my guide about asking the audience in the Zen center to vote between the Buddha and John Lennon. This was after reading an unloving text from the *Dhammapada* (included below in the Commentary section), and comparing it with Lennon's lyrics "All you need is love." John Lennon wins! That recollection was extremely funny to me, accompanied by much giggling. Then, I talked about the choice between the Muslim mystic Rumi (lots of love) and the Japanese Zen teacher Dogen (ugh) (see text below in the Commentary).

I also asked members of the Zen center audience to look around and say to the people near them, "You are my other self." (This comes from a Mayan greeting, "Inlakesh.") I then said, "You're practicing emptiness!" and the response I got was, "We are?" which seemed oh so funny, too, while on this psilocybin journey, a real knee-slapper. Instead of some abstract, highfalutin' idea of what the Buddhist term "emptiness" means, I was making the point that emptiness has no separation.

Later on in this journey, I commented more about Dogen, who wrote some awful, unloving words. I remember talking to Dogen as if he were in the room, saying something like, "You can't pretend those negative words were just a teaching trick. No way. I'm not letting you off the hook." That also seemed very funny.

Dogen was often snarky when he wrote about other people. Having just undergone what felt like a great deal of purification during this journey, I felt I understood, mystically or intuitively, what Dogen's problem was: although he had enlightenment experience and wrote plenty of wise texts, he wasn't fully purified.

From there, I began thinking of the Soto Zen Buddhist sect. I reflected on how they had other unresolved negative karma, specifically due to their complicity with the Japanese military during World War II. I spoke about this to my guide, saying that the sect still carries this burden, but it's hidden from public view.

These considerations about Soto Zen began a transition from the light-hearted to the heart-breaking. Journeys are so unpredictable, yet somehow find places you need to visit and heal.

After reflecting on how Soto Zen supported the Japanese military, the tattoo on the inside of the forearm of my sister-in-law's late stepfather came into my mind. I then spoke of this, and him, to my guide. The tattoo was the serial number given to him while a prisoner in Auschwitz. (He made a remarkable escape.) He was a wonderfully sweet man, not in any way bitter.

Then to the transpersonal! Suddenly I was transported to the darkest of experiences—the murder of myself and my family members. At least that's how I experienced it, as a past life. I witnessed and experienced the murder of my child-self (maybe age six or so) and both parents by gunfire at the hands of Nazi soldiers. It was winter; we were wearing heavy coats. We ran from the soldiers, but were cornered and shot. It was so real and gut-wrenchingly terrible and terrifying that I vomited (I had never vomited on a journey before). I remember calling out, "The horror!" and bursting into a torrent of tears.

In these mystical experiences, it is difficult to say who was there, being brutally murdered, and whether it was in fact my past life. However, in my journey, I was the child victim. I do sense it was my most recent past life.

Some background: I occasionally have had dreams where Nazi soldiers would threaten me and others and I needed to escape. I had interpreted this Nazi presence in my dreams as some sort of archetypal threat. However, now I believe differently: I was actually experiencing family trauma, and the Nazi soldiers were not mere archetypes. Ever since this journey, I have had no more dreams involving Nazi soldiers. I feel that I did experience and hopefully heal something real and hugely traumatic.

After this terrible and intense experience passed, I returned to my theme of growing as a bodhisattva. I was finally coming down from the strong medicine. I said to my guide, "I asked for it. Bring it on." That is, I asked for the purification and healing. And I asked to take on the pain and suffering; I would take on the family trauma too.

Wow! What an incredible journey into the mystery! From purifying in white light, to giggling about old, flawed Buddhist literature, to the reliving the horrors of murder by Nazis in my past life.

Often, we wonder how much can we take. I think it's like my guide said in his prayer for me at the start of the journey: "May Chris learn as much as he is ready to learn, heal as much as he is ready to heal, grow as much as he is ready to grow." The answer appears to be… we can take as much as we are ready for.

Commentary

This was an incredibly mind-altering journey. The transpersonal experience of being murdered was so real and shocking, not to mention beyond anything I'd imagined would possibly happen on this voyage. How to explain it? How would you explain it? Past life? Family trauma? My father's side of the family immigrated from current-day Belarus around 1900. Undoubtedly, there were distant relatives who died by Nazi hands. But the experience seemed so personal, so first-hand, so real and detailed. Not to mention horrific. Parents being murdered, too.

In contrast, the reflections on and insights into Buddhist teachings and teachers were foreshadowed in my ordinary waking life; after all, I had given a whole talk on the subject. However, my perspectives seemed to expand and were more enlivened in the journey space. I felt confident about my insights about the shortcomings of some Buddhist teachings and their lack of lovingkindness and human affection. For the record, to support my notions on the subject, here is some of the text from the *Dhammapada*.

In chapter 16, titled "Affection," (supposedly) the Buddha speaks thusly about love:

> *210. Seek no intimacy with the beloved... for not to see the beloved is painful.*

> *211. Therefore hold nothing dear, for separation from the dear is painful. There are no bonds for those who have nothing beloved.*

> *212. From endearment springs grief, from endearment springs fear. From him who is wholly*

*free from endearment there is no grief, when
then fear?*

*213. From affection springs grief, from affection
springs fear. From him who is wholly free from
affection there is no grief, when then fear?*

(Trans. Acharya Buddharakkhita)

Because this fundamental and early writing is attributed to
the Buddha himself, it is easy to understand why a great deal of
subsequent Buddhist literature and tradition convey a similarly
negative perspective on love and affection, and a positive perspective on asceticism.

This low view of affection, endearment, and intimacy has
persisted in the later development of Zen Buddhism. We can
see this in an example from the literature of the teacher Dogen
(born 1200 CE), the founder of the Japanese Soto sect of Zen
Buddhism. Dogen wrote a collection of essays known as the
Shobogenzo. In the chapter "On Ceaseless Practice," he says:

*Even though we prize our relationships, such
connections between ourselves and others are not
things that can be held onto, so if we do not let go of
our loved ones, chances are that our loved ones will
let go of us, both in word and in deed...*

Do not cling to love and affection, which is more foolish than the behavior of birds and beasts. Even if you are attached to feelings of love, they will not remain with you over the long years. (Gyōji)

(Trans. Rev. Hubert Nearman, O.B.C.)

Clearly, I'm not an apologist for these kinds of writings. And that's what I was expressing in my journey—calling them out, you might say. I felt the medicine flowing through me like a truth serum.

To reiterate briefly a point I wrote about in my prior book, one can interpret these un-loving Buddhist quotations as expressing the principle of non-attachment. However, a better way to interpret "non-attachment" is "unconditional," as in unconditional love. Great teachers like Rumi, and, yes, John Lennon spoke openly about the power of love and the gift of love. That's the direction my journey helped me affirm.

MONSTERS IN THE SHADOWS

Are you afraid to close your eyes
'cause monsters might appear?
Perhaps they do appear,
beings and places that eat you,
eat your soul, your flesh,
getting closer, then surround you.
Torture and untimely death,
the rack and thumb screw,
horses pulling arms and legs off,
dragging you in the dust,
arrows and spears piercing flesh,
burning huts and houses,
rescue out of reach.
This did happen, 'tis not a dream.
In the ocean of living,
predators and death lurk below,
appear from the murky distance.
Monsters in the shadows

10

MUSHROOM AND 5-MEO-DMT JOURNEY, OCTOBER 31, 2019 (HALLOWEEN)

Intentions

Please continue to purify, heal, and teach me, so I may grow as a bodhisattva.

May I be a channel of your love.

Thanks be to God!

Setting

Indoors, back in the same journey room as before; a solo journey with the same trusted guide. There was recorded music. A morning start.

From my guide's notes

My grandmother, warm love.

It's just love; love people as much as you can.

My Bubbe, my grandmother.

May I be a channel of your love.

Letting go of everything, people, children are hard to let go of, letting go of life, like a flower opens up to the sun, closes down, goes back to the earth.

The natural flow.

Grieving for <sister-in-law> diagnosed with lung cancer.

She gave so much for life, people; unconditional love.

Journey

As I've said before, each journey is unpredictable. Why would this one be any different?

I was uneasy in the days before my fifth psilocybin mushroom journey (five dried grams). I think it was primarily because my guide and I had planned to add a new element to the journey, namely a dose of the chemical 5-MeO-DMT ("5-MeO") to be insufflated (snorted) during the time when the mushroom's effects were still strong. Another step into the unknown! Another step in my exploration of consciousness and the cosmos, and another step in my education.

I had read a bit and listened to some videos of people reporting on their 5-MeO experience. They were mostly positive, although some were a bit worrisome. But none of the descriptions I read or listened to reported dosing within a five-gram mushroom journey. Yikes!

There also was stress for me because of my sister-in-law's very recent diagnosis of lung cancer. More stress than I realized beforehand, as will become clear. Her diagnosis was really fresh and her condition was not yet well diagnosed. My brother told us she had significant weight loss; she is already a diminutive person, so we were worried the cancer was advanced.

I don't think my anxiety had anything to do with the journey being scheduled on Halloween. Maybe a little? Seems funny. It wasn't helping calm me, anyhow.

The set and setting were similar to prior solo journeys. The altar was about the same (see photo). My guide and I came together as before, with beautiful ceremonial prayers and offerings in preparation for taking the sacrament of the plant medicine and entering the journey. I brought some dried sage from my garden as an additional offering. He lit a tightly wound bunch of sage he already had, and we used its smoke for smudging with special attention as part of our ritual.

My written intentions were open-ended and the same as for the last journey. I read them aloud during our ceremonial opening, and then added a prayer of support and love for my sister-in-law.

We reviewed the plan for the day, which began at 10 AM. The plan included taking the 5-MeO. We spoke of technique, how to take in the medicine by gentle insufflation. Also, he mentioned that he would help me go to the bathroom before the dose, as you don't want to be uncomfortable or even wet yourself during the 5-MeO experience. This was a review, as we had covered this ground during our fifty-minute preparation session a few days before.

My guide then put on some music and left me alone to consume the five dried grams of mushrooms that we had agreed on. This was a bit lower weight than what I had taken in the prior journey. I felt that five grams would be plenty strong enough, especially considering that it was in some ways serving as a base for the further experience of the 5-MeO. (That really wasn't a good way to look at it, though, as I appreciate now. The mushroom medicine had its own major role in the experience. This was essentially two separate journeys.)

Sitting up on my round, black meditation cushion that I had brought, I ate the dried mushrooms in the traditional Mexican manner. A little honey helped the eating, which took perhaps twenty minutes or so. As before, I could feel the effects just starting to come on while I was finishing the mushrooms. My guide returned right around that time.

I believe he changed the music; and I put on my eyeshade and slipped under the covers on the thin but comfortable mattress lying on the floor. My guide took notes, recording what I had to say.

The music was perfectly tailored to the beginning of a journey. It opened gently with pleasant major chords, but slowly morphed into minor dissonant chords in concert with my changing consciousness.

As the medicine's effect strengthened, I had significant chills and shivering. This is a known occasional side-effect of the mushrooms. It also is a way to release stored body trauma energy. I asked for an extra blanket, which my guide supplied.

He told me not to worry about the shivers; go ahead and shiver away. I did, letting the shivering be as intense as it wanted to be; and after some time, it tapered off.

As the shivers waned and my guide played some romantic classical music, a memory of warm love entered me and flowed through my veins. I thought of my Bubbe, my Jewish paternal grandmother, who always seemed warm and loving to me. (She died of cancer when I was about eight years old, so my memories are only from childhood.)

Feelings of love moved me to say, "It's just love. Love people as much as you can."

As the medicine further intensified, I felt a strong swirling energy, accompanied by images and feelings about my Bubbe who represented unconditional love and warmth, my newly diagnosed sister-in-law who represented the same unselfish caring and nurturing energy, and my ninety-six-year-old mother who was emotionally absent. This was compounded by the fact that at the time, my mother was living with my sister-in-law and my oldest brother. It was here in the journey that a rough dissonance burst forth between loving warmth and cold cancer. I was tossed about in the Celestial Washing Machine with a feminine earth mixture of love and death, life and pain.

About this time, I told my guide that I didn't want to do the 5-MeO that day. He said okay. (After the journey, I told him that at that point, I felt like a prize fighter who cried "¡No mas!" to his manager.) I think this may have been the most challenging, trying moment of all my journey experiences up until then.

I know I was in the Celestial Washing Machine's agitator for a long time, trying to come to peace with the cancer associated with love and nurture, and coldness contrasted with vibrant health. The prospect of an additional unknown but potentially earth-shattering jolt from the 5-MeO seemed just too much, and I think eliminating that from the back of my mind made me relax a little.

Eventually, my struggle eased, the apparent conflict and irony softened, and I spoke: "May I be a channel of your love."

I also said, "Letting go of everything, people… children are hard to let go of… letting go of life… like a flower opens up to the sun, closes down and goes back to the earth… the natural flow."

It felt like there was much time spent in this part of the journey with the mystery, beauty and tragedy, feminine nature, and life and death.

My guide then asked me if I would take the 5-MeO now. Although I felt more peaceful, I told him I still had some apprehension. He said, "I think it will take you to a different space." I pondered for a moment, and told him that I trusted him and would do it.

I took off my eyeshades so I could walk, and he led me to the bathroom and left me alone to pee. He then led me back to the mattress, and I put my eyeshades back on while sitting up. In preparation for the insufflation, he had me blow my nose and check which nostril was clearer. He had me close one nostril with a finger and gently inhale through a tube through my other nostril, and then gently exhale through my mouth. I did this three times. 5-MeO is extremely potent, and I inhaled a very small amount of material, probably only about twenty mg in total.

I lay back down, and my guide put on some gentle music. The onset was quick, five or ten minutes. And then... Wow!! Talk about a different space! The reader will have to understand that it's a struggle to try to describe the ineffable.

I floated up and merged into a sky of white light. An incredible feeling of peace permeated all, was all. There was no time, no you or me. No anything. But it was something, the most amazing, wonderful, beautiful something. As best I can tell, this wasn't like heaven, this *was* heaven. I was transported to heaven, given a gift of wonderment, an experience of pure love and peace. A blessing.

And God knows I needed it. Thank you, God! After my struggle coming to peace with gyrating feelings about Bubbe, my sister-in-law, and my mother, I was psychically exhausted.

I had no sense of time during my 5-MeO journey, but in earth time, it was probably about sixty minutes. I floated down. Gently, peacefully, lovingly.

The 5-MeO effect had diminished. The mushroom's effects were still present, but also diminishing. With my eyeshades now off, I had a few minutes of spontaneous crying. My guide asked why the tears. I told him, "Grieving for my sister-in-law and her family. She gave so much for life, for people. She didn't care about getting something in return. Unconditional love." Better to let out that grief than hold it in.

As the crying subsided, the journey came to an end.

Amazing! The Celestial Washing Machine helped me better come to peace with the death of beautiful, giving people, people I love. The lifting of the flower toward the sun and its withering and falling back to the earth. With heaven above, always there. Nothing to fear.

Glory to God!

Commentary

Again, this was an incredibly mind-altering journey. Why should I expect anything else?

Certainly, it was a journey of great contrasts. Part of the mushroom journey felt physically and psychically exhausting— the part about the warmth of life giving way to the coldness of death, the flower blossoming and folding in. This experience was deep teaching about letting go, about the cycle of life and death.

In contrast, and just as monumental, was my first experience with 5-MeO and how I came to accept it. Although my guide and I had decided ahead of time that I would partake during the mushroom experience, in the moment, I tried to back out. I feared the unknown of the 5-MeO experience, and fretted that I was just being worn out. And yet, with knowledge and intuition, and in a patient and noncoercive way, my guide led me to this new medicine. The reward was a wonderful experience of the divine, as well as relief from my earlier struggles that day.

A word about safety. The 5-MeO medicine is strong and following the wisdom of my guide and his teachers, should not be provided to journeyers who are inexperienced. Rather the journeyer should have already demonstrated the ability to journey with mushrooms and to have done so in a stable, safe manner. An initial dose should not be too big. This follows upon the guidance that, under most circumstances, mushrooms should only be offered after the journeyer has shown the ability to stably handle the MDMA experience.

11

GROUP MUSHROOM AND 5-MEO-DMT JOURNEY, DECEMBER 2019

Intentions

To grow as a bodhisattva and learn.

Setting

A house in the San Francisco Bay Area; wintertime. An afternoon start, with a sleepover. An altar. No recorded music, but plenty of singing.

Journey

This was a group journey—ten journeyers, our guide, and three assistants, with magic mushrooms for all. Although they didn't play any recorded music, the leaders and assistants sang periodically, and toward the end of the event, some of us journeyers also sang. It was good to see people whom I journeyed with last summer. It also was good to meet some new people—and while maybe I felt a bit distant from them at the beginning, by the end of the journey we were all one big family, a love fest, really.

We met around 3 PM. As is customary, we started by doing some group activities. After taking turns giving brief individual introductions, our first activity was to share our intentions. Mine were to grow as a bodhisattva and to learn.

Then we had another opportunity to get to know each other more, to engage in some group bonding. This was fun, too. We all stood in a circle, and took turns inviting all those of a certain background to briefly step into the middle. The guide-leader began the exercise saying, "Everyone who was born outside the U.S., come into the circle." Next, someone said, "Everyone born in the Midwest, come into the circle." Other prompts included "Everyone who plays a musical instrument," "Everyone who speaks a language in addition to English," and so on.

Next, we prayed to the seven directions. These are the four cardinal directions, plus Above, Below, and Center. It went like this… whoever started for that direction would shake the rattle and speak to the spirit(s) of that direction. They might invoke the spirit and ask for guidance and protection, while expressing gratitude and praising its character. Then, others in the group would join the invocation, naming more characteristics of that particular direction. We took turns initiating the prayers, passing the ceremonial rattle. We started with West, perhaps because the winter sun was beginning to go down. We all faced west, our guide opened the invocation, and others in the group uttered phrases like "Direction of sunset" and "Our shadows." I started the direction Above. This prayer was both a dedication and an opening ritual.

For our next group activity, our guide had us chant "om mani padme hum," and then led us in a discussion of what this Buddhist mantra meant. He gave us a handout that showed how each of the six syllables corresponds to one of six paramitas (Buddhist noble characteristics), and what personal flaw or struggle each of those paramitas purifies. Part of that table is reproduced below.

SYLLABLES	PARAMITAS	PURIFIES
Om	Generosity	Pride / Ego
Man	Ethics	Jealousy
Ni	Patience	Passion / Desire
Pad	Diligence	Ignorance / Prejudice
Me	Renunciation	Greed
Hum	Wisdom	Aggression / Hatred

Then we paired up. Our guide suggested we get together with somebody whom we weren't familiar with; I joined the gentleman sitting next to me. We were given a blank sheet of paper. Before we started talking to each other, we were instructed to draw the flaw selected from the third column of the "om mani padme hum" table that we most needed to purify.

I drew two people, simple character forms, one colored yellow and one orange, semi-obscured behind a gray cloud.

The issue I chose to purify was ignorance / prejudice. I told my partner about a dream I'd had where I saw people clearly, but they were somehow nameless. I reasoned that clearing away the cloud in my drawing would symbolize identifying my own ignorance and understanding my own prejudice. Ultimately, my drawing really was about accepting people just the way they are.

My motivation for this diligent work? It is part of my ongoing effort to stay aware of all my prejudices as they come up, as much as I can, and remind myself to be present, nonjudgmental, and nonreactive, which is a practice of mindfulness.

Then, it was my partner's turn. His drawing was basically solid blackness. There was no life to it; a deadness covered the whole piece of paper. He told me he knew what he needed to purify but it wasn't in the table or on the handout. He needed to work on guilt. Guilt was terrifying for him, and debilitating, extremely debilitating. He talked about how guilt was ingrained in his Catholic family of origin. It was a good lesson for me, for a couple of reasons. It made me realize the limitations of the table and the dogma for understanding the "om mani padme hum" mantra. Where was "guilt" in the chart? I also realized that the burden my partner was carrying clearly was more oppressive than what I was carrying at this point in my journey. We talked about what might be a good paramita for guilt. I suggested wisdom: the wisdom to be aware of guilt, to know that guilt wasn't his own material but rather material someone else had dumped on him. He seemed to like the idea.

Next, we all lay our pieces of paper in the middle of the circle. We moved clockwise slowly around them while we chanted "om mane padme hum," looking carefully at each drawing as we passed it.

Then, we set up for the evening, bringing out our pads and sleeping bags. I foolishly had brought only a thin yoga mat for the hardwood floor, so I was pretty uncomfortable. We arranged our mats like the spokes of a wheel. It was cozy with ten of us in the living room, not a lot of space between some of the mats.

It was now dark outside with the early sunset, near winter solstice. We each came up to get some of the medicine. I received my five grams of dried mushrooms, along with a few cocoa beans and a little honey, on a small paper plate. We waited until everybody got their medicine, and then we ate. I was the last one to finish.

I had a pretty peaceful mushroom journey, relatively speaking; it was mostly centered on love. I just tried to stay focused on love and my breath. Before too long, my neighbor began having a very difficult journey. The same thing had happened at my last group journey—the person next to me had the hardest time. The guides attended to her and comforted her. I could pick up her pain; felt compassion. My journey wasn't as notable as prior journeys, or maybe I just didn't bring a lot of memories back. Perhaps the mushroom medicine decided that I needed an easy experience.

At some point during the latter half of the mushroom journey, our guide came over and asked if I was ready to try the

5-MeO (I was the only one in our group who was going to do this). I said yes. One of the assistants took me to the bathroom. I peed, came back, blew my nose, put my eyeshades back on, and inhaled maybe three times through my left nostril, insufflating the powder.

This was my second experience with this medicine. The last time, it was like being taken to heaven. This time was different. One lesson I've learned is that you can never predict how a journey will go, so don't bother trying.

My expectations for this second 5-MeO journey had been pretty concrete, but it didn't happen the way I had planned. Instead, it was like I reached into the heavenly cookie jar for another heaven cookie, but before I could get it... my hand got slapped. The message—the teaching—I received was that I needed to learn more about unconditional love, and that when God means unconditional, she means *unconditional!* There is no wiggle room. It's absolute, and even the littlest bit of a condition contaminates the well. It has to be totally pure. None of this *I'll scratch your back and you scratch mine.* No expectations.

Unlike the mushroom part of the journey, my 5-MeO experience was intense. In fact, it kicked my ass. The medicine put me in my place; or more likely, the Divine or the helper spirits did, through the medicine. This part probably lasted about one hour. I don't remember my neighbor crying, or even being in my body.

After the end of everyone's mushroom journey time, the bell rang and there was more singing, and a snack was served.

We journeyers had a little time to sit close together and talk as we ate. A friend shared a bigger portable mattress they had brought, so I didn't have to sleep on the yoga mat all night.

Commentary

The unpredictable, once again. This time, the mushroom journey was peaceful and focused on love, while the 5-MeO journey was taxing. I was taken to task, also about love—at the highest standard, totally unconditional. No wiggle room! A work in progress to be sure.

Group journeys have their own special character. There's a group healing and growing energy. It reminds me of what my first Zen teacher Seung Sahn used to say about why it's helpful to practice in groups. He said it's like washing potatoes. The way you wash lots of potatoes is to put them all together in water and then agitate them; they bump up against each other and knock the dirt off. Certainly, the Celestial Washing Machine has an agitator.

12

GROUP MDMA JOURNEY, JANUARY 2020

Intentions

Develop more unconditional love and patience.
May I grow as a bodhisattva. Thanks be to God.

Setting

San Francisco Bay Area house; day-time journey (no sleepover); our guide, one assistant, and six journeyers, including myself. Live music, singing, and poetry readings.

Journey

This workshop had a theme: Connection and Friendship.

We gathered in a circle and shared our introductions and intentions. After an opening prayer, we each took a capsule containing MDMA. My dose was 150 mg.

We lay down onto our mats and put on our eyeshades. For the first hour of the workshop, we embarked on individual journeys. Sometimes there was quiet. Sometimes the guide and the assistant sang songs or read poems. One of the poems was the famous "When Death Comes" by Mary Oliver. Another was a not-as-well-known poem by N. Peck, transcribed below; it's a favorite of mine, now.

During this hour, I allowed thoughts and feelings to wash over me as waves of energy rushed through.

I reflected on my mother, who was approaching her death. I was coming to peace with her passing. (She would die later in 2021, at age ninety-eight.) I reflected on other relationships, as well.

Then, our guide told us to slowly come out of our individual journeys, take off our eyeshades, and sit up. When everyone was ready, he instructed us to partner with another participant for the next phase of the journey. I paired up with a middle-aged man who was sitting next to me.

My partner and I sat closely facing each other. In a natural and spontaneous move, he held out his hands for me to hold, which I found a beautiful and thoughtful opening. I could feel how warm his hands were, somewhat sweaty from the medicine. He had taken a booster dose and had more MDMA in his system than I did. We were both at the peak of the medicine.

We were asked to address the following questions, one at a time and taking turns for each:

- ♦ Who are you?
- ♦ How do I connect to myself?
- ♦ How do I connect to others?

♦ What is friendship for me?

We each shared our answers, looking into the other's eyes, still holding hands, with whatever came into consciousness, not thinking it over. I most vividly remember my response to the question, "Who are you?" I answered: "I am the divine manifested in this body."

There were other beautiful things uttered by both of us, but I don't remember the words. The feelings were of love and openness.

All six of us then came together in a circle and shared with the group some of what we had shared in pairs, as well as reflected on our experiences as a whole. Then, we ate a delicious meal.

Commentary

Connection and Friendship. That's also the foundation of Community.

This was an unusual MDMA experience, particularly the pairing. Some of the individuals in the other pairs knew each other somewhat, or even a lot. I myself had never met this man before that day. And yet, with the help of the medicine and a safe container, this was an intimate experience for all of us. A comfortable and emotional one, too.

Sometimes, romantic couples journey together with MDMA. Sometimes with a therapist-guide and sometimes just by themselves. With a therapist-guide, the format can be similar: namely, spending the first hour in individual journeys, and then coming together as a pair. There may be some issues they have decided ahead of time to work on. But often, there is no prior agenda, just an opportunity to spontaneously share and be together with the heart-opening medicine.

This was an experiment in connection and friendship. A successful one.

HUMAN PRAYER

I dedicate my body,
child of the earth,
To the sacred work,
So that I might always feel
The wisdom of the path.

I dedicate my mind,
mirror of the sky,
To the sacred work,
So that I might always know
The nature of the path.

I dedicate this breath,
spirit of the air,
To the sacred work,
So that I might always hear
The teachings of the path.

I dedicate my friendships,
forest of life,
To the sacred work,
So that I might always live
The purpose of the path.

I dedicate my nature,
beloved self,
To the sacred work,
So that I might always remember
The path is love.

by N. Peck

13

Mushroom and Ketamine Journey in the Redwood Forest, May 2020

Intentions

Please continue to purify, heal, and teach me, so I may grow as a bodhisattva.
Please take me on a learning journey, and may I bring back much that I've experienced and learned.
May I be a channel of your love. Thanks be to God!

Setting

A small clearing in a secluded redwood forest in the San Francisco Bay Area; daytime; my usual guide. Tarp, pad, sleeping bag, eyeshades. A simple altar set up on the ground, on top of a pretty Mexican cloth covering the redwood needles.

From my guide's notes

Being with people, letting go. Being like a grandfather.
Letting the medicine work, cleaning me up, processing…

Letting go of rules and expectations.

Letting go of how things need to be.

Try not to do too much. Enjoy what I have.

Important thing is not hurting anybody.

The earth wants me back at some point.

[with the ketamine]: Peace, love, family.

Journey

There was a gap in time between my prior journey and this one, due to the uncertainty coming with the outbreak of COVID-19. Also, it felt more comfortable—safer—to journey outdoors during a pandemic. I took five and a half grams of dried mushrooms, and an additional 110 mg of ketamine administered by intramuscular injection sometime later, essentially creating two journeys.

It is always a special opportunity to journey outside. Nature played an important role in the day's experience, no surprise.

The big themes were letting go and accepting. You could say that these would always be good themes, and you would be right. But the feeling deep inside was especially strong this time.

My guide's notes showed that my thoughts and feelings of "letting go" began right away. But also interesting was my statement about being like a grandfather. At this time, my daughter was pregnant with her first child, my first grandchild. I also was sixty-eight years old and feeling into my elder role—a role of tolerance and love, sharing with others whatever wisdom and gifts I have to offer.

It was not unusual for my guide to check in with me—"How are you doing?"—and for me to respond, "I'm cleaning." Yes, the Celestial Washing Machine cleans.

Letting go, letting go, letting go. Letting go of just about everything, like rules and expectations, how things need to be. This causes a great relaxation of body-mind.

At some point, I could feel the weight of my body being pulled down by the earth. I deeply felt my mortality and commented that the earth wants me back at some point. Subsequently, I told my kids that when I die, my preferred way to handle my body is to turn it into compost.

Enlightenment is being intimate with all things, said one teacher. Later, still with eyeshades on, I lay with my arms outstretched and my hands extended a little ways beyond the tarp. I touched the ground with my hands and picked up some of the forest floor. My hands explored the feeling of the earth—redwood needles, twigs, dirt. Beautiful feeling of oneness. Psychically, spiritually, I was one with the earth, deeply connected. I felt intimate with all things.

A famous Buddhist image is that of the Buddha touching the earth as his witness at the moment of his enlightenment. I reflected on this image after my journey and came up with another interpretation: the Buddha was simply being one with the earth.

My cosmic awareness was that everything is perfect just as it is. That is, a sense of true acceptance. A fly came by and buzzed around for a little bit. Perfect buzzing fly. Moments later, I decided to take off my eyeshades. I saw a very young redwood tree, just a few feet tall, trying to make its way in the world, so young and vibrantly green with a dead brown branch from another tree leaning against it—perfect, just like that.

Then, my guide played an ocarina. I decided to stand up. I'm not sure if that was before or after the ketamine. No matter. I recall taking a few steps and turning my body toward a big red-wood tree; suddenly, I was standing right next to an extremely large brown horse. I felt the power of this horse, way powerful, majestic. Clearly a spiritual appearance. I realized this horse is my spirit animal. Amazing!

One does not need to interpret such an appearance, but a horse represents swiftness, strength, enlightenment, healing, and forward movement. The attending photo is of a small wood carving of a horse by a Native American that sits on my altar.

Commentary

What an awesome, huge journey!

Being intimate with all things. In other words, accepting everything just as it is. No grasping, no struggle, no desire. The perfection of a buzzing fly and the dead branch against the young green sapling. Being one with the earth.

A Buddhist might say this represents nonattachment, but I think it better expressed as *absolute attachment*, perfection of oneness. Connection. Great Peace.

Topped off by the magical appearance of my spirit animal. So magnificent!

Thank you, thank you, thank you.

14

Ayahuasca Journey, July 2020

Intentions

Please show me this Amazonian medicine's character.
Help me, please; connect me with the spirit world so I may better help others.
Let go of trying to control or judge people and circumstances, and accept all people just the way they are now.

Setting

A house in the San Francisco Bay Area; an experienced guide.

Journey

I had heard much about ayahuasca, so I sought out an opportunity to experience the medicine myself. My guide this day was an acquaintance of my regular guide. He was well-versed with the medicine, having spent years in the Amazonian jungle at an ayahuasca healing retreat center. Most ayahuasca journeys are done in a group setting, but because of COVID-19, this guide was offering individual journeys for the time being.

We began outside, practicing ceremonial cleaning with tobacco water—water that had been soaked with mapacho tobacco from South America. My guide poured some of this water into my cupped hands. I then quickly brought the liquid up to my nose and inhaled sharply, simultaneously raising my head so that the tobacco water traveled into my sinuses. Wow! Not particularly pleasant, to say the least, but it certainly gave me a rush and brought energy into my head.

We went inside to begin the ceremony. After a prayer, the guide and I both drank a small glass of the ayahuasca liquid. This liquor was from Hawaii and made from only the two primary plants, no extras. It was thick and viscous, a dark chocolate brown, and it had a somewhat pleasant earth taste.

I was a bit surprised that my guide drank as much of the brew as I did, a full dose, but that's how it is often done with this medicine.

As the medicine took effect, the guide beautifully sang traditional Peruvian Amazon ayahuasca songs, known as icaros, to call the medicine spirits, and shook two shakapa instruments, special bundles of leaves that make a rustling sound. The songs were central to the ceremony and experience.

The medicine was powerful. For about three or four hours, it was a full-on journey. I had visions of spirits. It reminded me of a good mushroom journey, but with a slightly different character.

One spirit vision in particular was of a figure wearing what looked like a headdress made of two feathers. I somehow interpreted this figure as being Quetzalcoatl, even though that god is from Mesoamerican traditions, not from South America where the ayahuasca drink originated. So what did *that* mean? As an aside, two years later I was on a group tour at Teotihuacan, an ancient city close to Mexico City. There, in front of the temple of Quetzalcoatl, a Toltec teacher gave me the ceremonial name Teohuicatl ("boy of the rain of the sky"). So Quetzalcoatl resonates for me.

Perhaps the biggest difference from mushroom journeys is the purging ayahuasca brings. My experience was a bit unusual, just dry heaves, which didn't start until after three or four hours, when I was in my descent. They were unpleasant! Lasted a good half hour, which is a long time for that. I guess I had a bunch of toxic stuff to unload! Although I wonder if the nausea isn't just the physiological response. Anyhow, it felt like with each dry heave, there was an associated specific mistake or piece of bad karma I was releasing, although I wasn't having any specific images or memories.

The next day, I was very tired. The day after that, I felt refreshed and especially peaceful. A challenging but rewarding experience!

Commentary

I wanted to experience medicine work from a different tradition. Mission accomplished! Not that I now know everything about the ayahuasca medicine and its rituals, but this was certainly a good introduction. Although I am content with the medicines I had experienced before, I am glad to expand my world. There will be more journeys with ayahuasca.

This was a spiritual journey with visions of spirits and what felt like a purging of bad habits, or bad karma. The connection with Quetzalcoatl was also prominent.

Growing and healing—step by step.

TWO FEATHERS

Spirit with two-feathered crown, two-feathered
    headdress,
Who are you?
Where do you come from?
Why do I call you Quetzalcoatl?
Feathered deity of Mesoamerica
in an Amazonian ceremony.
I read two feathers decorated
the crown of Egyptian god Amun.
Perhaps others, too

Maybe you are none or all the above,
this visitation, so mysterious,
no business cards or
trumpeted announcements

Beyond name?
And what is that form?

More mysteries to come…
Perhaps one day, one journey,
I will understand identities
if that's even a relevant concept

Until then, gratitude, curiosity,
communion, connection
are all embraceable.
May they visit again

15

Mushroom Journey, August 2020

Intentions

Please take me on a healing and learning journey, and may
I bring back much that I've experienced.
May I heal self-doubt and feelings that I'm not lovable.
Please help me be of service to others.
May I be a channel of your love. Thanks be to God!

Setting

A house in the San Francisco Bay Area; my regular, trusted guide. Music playing on speakers. Eyeshades, as always. A
comfortable mat, covers.

From my guide's notes

This is good for me, opening me up.
I'm feeling the mother spirit.
Healing, purifying, thank you.

[with bodywork] Let the fathers out, let the fathers go. I don't need them. Let the fathers go, let the fathers go to God. Get out of me!

I'm the path.

Journey

This was a mushroom journey, five and a half grams.

In this journey, I had the spiritual experience of being in the presence of the Divine Mother. Hers was a celestial mothering presence, a completely loving mother spirit who communicated to me that I am totally lovable and totally loved. She appeared as a big spirit in size, gentle but powerful, warm, accepting and compassionate. What a blessing! Especially for one who was not given that deep sense of welcome in his early days. What a profoundly healing and purifying experience! Thank you!

Later in the journey, my guide offered me some bodywork, as he sometimes did. I accepted, and at one point he applied some gentle pressure on my thighs, my quadriceps. A great cathartic response erupted:

Let the fathers out, let the fathers go. I don't need them.

Let the fathers go, let the fathers go to God. Get out of me!

This was a release of the toxic male, the toxic paternal that had infiltrated my body. How infiltrated? Probably in multiple ways. In some intergenerational, transpersonal way for sure, and also culturally, too. My voice was loud and clear, with a crescendo to a great emphatic shout of "Get out of me!"

I believe my "go to God" cry signified that before God, the Toxic Fathers would meet their justice or be released—or at least, they would no longer be present in me. After this release, I heard my guide spitting out poison in the bathroom.

Later still in the journey, I uttered, "I'm the path." That did not mean that I think I am special, however. It is synonymous with being *on* the path, with an understanding of unity.

As I came down from the medicine and settled into resting, I reflected that a lot of good work had happened. Good trouble! This "get out of me!"

Commentary

What a marvelous healing journey! Big; huge! With a fascinating juxtaposition of the Divine Mother and the Toxic Father! This is not to say all fathers are toxic—far from that. But I was blessed in two wonderful ways in this journey: with the love of the Divine Mother and the release of much male toxicity!

Thanks be to God!

AM I WORTHY?

What a question!
Many doubt or wonder.
Is worthiness something to be earned?
Perhaps why we've come to earth,
like a hero's journey?
Or a birthright?

16

Mushroom and Ketamine Journey in a Redwood Forest, October 2020

Intentions

Please take me on a spiritual journey.
May I feel I am enough, I am complete.
May I relax and let things be in their own way. Neither self
nor other-than-self.
Please help me be of service to others. May I be a channel
of your love. Thanks be to God!

Setting

A redwood forest in the San Francisco Bay Area; daytime.
Tarp, pad, sleeping bag, eyeshades—the usual for outdoors. My
trusted guide. Outdoor altar (see photo).

From my guide's notes

[with mushrooms]
Medicine is cleaning me out.

My mother is dying.

Clearing doubt that I am good enough, that I'm complete.

Accept my imperfections, being human.

Let God into my heart, love other people.

The purpose of life is simply to love people.

Let other people help, learning how to let go, letting be.

The smell of the forest is wonderful.

[with ketamine]

I went to the ocean.

I float! I would sink when I was a kid; now I float.

I'm swimming in the ocean.

Visions of healing family, the human family.

Journey

This was another big journey, beginning with six grams of dried mushrooms and culminating with 120 mg of ketamine administered via intramuscular injection.

As the notes indicate, the journey opened with a sensation of being cleaned by the Celestial Washing Machine.

After this, I reflected on my mother, who was in the later stages of her life. She would pass on August 8 the following year, on portal day, numerically 8/8.

Then there was a gentle feeling of self-acceptance—of being complete, good enough. Also of opening up—letting others in and letting go of whatever I was holding. Such a beautiful, healing, and growing path! Although I had had similar experiences in previous journeys, today's made me realize that multiple journeys are necessary for great transformation. There is a more complete, deeper psychic and spiritual reception with each new experience.

I sometimes say that these journeys are mostly about letting go and opening up, letting go and opening up, letting go and opening up... Rinse, repeat in the Celestial Washing Machine.

How sweet the statement *The purpose of life is simply to love people*. And add to that—all beings and things. We humans naturally look for meaning. After surviving the Holocaust, Victor Frankl developed the philosophy of logotherapy, positing that even in the midst of suffering, people can find meaning and purpose in their lives. What a simple and powerful life purpose the medicine revealed: to love everyone!

And to love nature, be one with nature! This was reflected in my comment *The smell of the forest is wonderful*. Journeying in nature is truly special. We generally use eyeshades when journeying, even outdoors, but the connection with nature is still strong. (Eyeshades help us have an inward journey. Our visual field can be so distracting. However, there is time to remove eyeshades in this approach, often toward the later stage of the outdoor journey.)

Next came the ketamine medicine, while still journeying with the mushrooms. 120 mg by intramuscular injection is a substantial dose, generally enough to drop the ego for most people. On this day, I had a marvelous spiritual experience!

As the notes show, I journeyed to the ocean. This was truly memorable. I found myself well below the sea surface, but not all the way down on the ocean floor. Instead, I just floated at a depth, mostly looking up toward the surface. The sensation of buoyancy was remarkable, especially given that ordinarily, my body sinks quickly, even in salty ocean water.

But this was no ordinary ocean experience. This was an ocean of consciousness and a sea of creation. From my comfortable dwelling place below the surface, I saw beings formed, coming together and drifting upward toward the surface where presumably they would take life. But they did not appear in physical bodies, like the ones you and I have. This was an ocean where spirit (or soul) was coming up from the depths to begin transforming into new life. I was given the gift of witnessing creation. A magical vision, whatever it was. Mysterious, for sure.

Eventually, I returned to my body in the redwood forest. A sense of healing peace permeated me. It was something about the transformation I witnessed, and maybe all that earlier letting go and accepting my and everyone's basic goodness, worthiness of love. Healing the human family.

Commentary

Water. Gentle water. Soft and flexible, water flows. Water is life, for forests and beings. From cleansing raindrops to the great ocean. From the individual path to collective consciousness and the sea of creation. Gentle healing rain of love and acceptance. Creation of life in the universal waters.

17

Mushroom and 5-MeO-DMT Journey, March 2021

Intentions

With awareness and understanding –
May I be healed as I let God teach me to heal.
May I heal others as I let God teach me to heal others.
May my heart open wide to the mystery and be filled with love.

Setting

A house in the San Francisco Bay Area; daytime; familiar room, music on speakers, eyeshades on, with my usual guide. We added sound healing to this journey, incorporating many different musical instruments.

From my guide's notes

Conflict. I want everything to be peaceful, but must accept when it is not.

I am cared for, I'm loved. I'm healing.
Trust the world, myself, God, others.

Journey

I began this journey by ingesting five and a half grams of dried magic mushrooms, followed by insufflating approximately twenty-five mg of 5-MeO (synthetic) crystal powder sometime during the latter part of the experience.

This was a pretty quiet mushroom journey; I didn't do very much speaking. But actually, speaking isn't a good metric of a journey's significance. And although I didn't verbalize as much this time as I had previously, I received profound truth. "Accepting" was the big theme. Trust goes hand in hand with accepting.

I accepted where I was on the path, and I was able to let go of expectations. I felt energized and happy during this part of the journey. I felt cared for and loved.

Later, as I was landing from the journey and still awash in these big feelings, I jotted down a contemplative list of the things that I was accepting. I decided to write using my non-dominant hand. This technique can help open up more of the psyche, and the whole brain. My list is reproduced at the end of this chapter.

My guide offered a lot of sound healing during this journey. He played many different musical instruments, and he placed tuning forks and bells onto my body, which gladly received the vibrations. There were so many different sounds! It was quite a treat. (When I took my eyeshades off at the very end of the journey, I was surprised that the room was strewn with so many instruments and sound makers of one sort or another. It made me appreciate how much skill this deliberate therapeutic approach takes.)

Then it was time for the 5-MeO, as I entered the latter part of the mushroom journey.

A vision appeared. There was a mystical trail—or perhaps a river—of souls, of spirits. I could see them moving. I realized this was a vista of past lives. How or where they were being transported, I couldn't say, but I was deeply moved, awestruck. I could see these souls individually, although they had no human shape. They were at some distance. I had an inkling that they were transitioning from one form of existence to another. Perhaps they were souls newly released from human bodies? Perhaps they were souls headed back to human bodies? I don't know. I do know the vision was breathtaking.

At some point, coming back into my body, I realized there was a pain in my heart. Not an overwhelming pain, but a distinct discomfort, a sharpness. It wasn't a welcome visitor, but there it was. I tried to stay curious, to gauge what it was telling me.

As I was feeling into this pain, I suddenly contacted a field of suffering—the suffering of many others. Tears streamed from my eyes and I grieved deeply for their pain.

Was this connected to my vision of the river of souls?

Commentary

Some journeys are so big that it's almost impossible to describe them. My words here seem small and few, relative to the experience itself: *I saw a river of souls.*

But it is a blessing to be given a mystical vision. I honor the gift, with much gratitude. And it's okay not to understand all that is shown.

This was another journey where transpersonal grieving surfaced, accompanied by deep crying. There will be more. There is much to grieve for in human life and over the course of human history. I honor connecting with this suffering. And although it was painful to experience, a beautiful release accompanied my deep crying. A healing, and not just for myself.

Last but not least… from the start of the journey to its conclusion, there was *acceptance*. If I am to accept all things, why not with kindness?

Accepting with

kindness...

love
everything
Nancy
fear
grasping
patience
not reacting
death
birth
sexuality
gratitude
past trauma
forgiveness
past lives
other people
teachers
other beings
sense of self and separateness
being one with the universe
trust
faith
being cared for
caring for others
pain
suffering   goodness

18

Group MDMA and Mushroom Journey in the Redwood Forest, May 2021

Intentions

[First night] May I have an open, loving heart, accepting all with kindness. May I carry that forward into daily life.
[Second night] Please let me meet one or more ancestral healers. May they teach me and support me.
May the forest wisdom teach me.

Setting

A redwood forest in the San Francisco Bay Area; tarp, camping pad, sleeping bag, eyeshade.

Journey

Our group of nine participants (including myself), our guide, and three assistants assembled at noontime on Friday. The ceremonies took place at night, beginning at sunset, and we finished around noon on Sunday. We slept outdoors. As customary for my guide's group journeys, there was a theme. The theme for this weekend gathering was green woman/green man or green person. This description signifies connecting to our natural roots, connecting with nature—appropriate for this forest gathering.

In addition to an MDMA journey the first evening (150 mg for me) and dried psilocybin mushrooms the second night (six grams), there were theme-related activities during the daytime.

We set up our site on Friday afternoon. The first activity was to work in silence to build a group altar out of the forest material. We naturally blended and built upon everyone's contributions and created a lovely piece. We used fallen branches to construct the skeleton of the structure, decorating it in creative ways with finer forest materials. Our guide and assistants participated, too.

After building the altar, our guides gave us face paints and a couple hand mirrors for a fun activity. They encouraged us to decorate our faces with the paints, as well as adorn our bodies with forest materials. I've included a (not-great-quality) photo of myself at the end of the chapter. I got compliments on my green eyebrows, although unfortunately they don't show well in the photo. There was much laughter, and we all looked wild indeed—some even wilder than me.

As sunset approached, we took the MDMA medicine. Although there is not a lot of detail for me to report from this first night's journey, I remember it being exceptionally peaceful.

I spent time reviewing several relationships, and love flowed through my body and spirit. It was beautiful being in the forest with my friends, our guide, and our friendly assistants.

The second day, after breakfast, we gathered in a circle and shared about our experiences the night before. We talked more about the theme of connecting to nature, being part of nature. We received a handout of Mary Oliver's famous poem "Wild Geese" (copied below), and we discussed in detail the poem's meaning and significance.

In the afternoon, our guides sent us out into the woods to spend several hours alone in the natural world. We were instructed to locate a place that felt energetically welcoming, and draw a circle around the area, with a diameter of five or ten meters. We were to remain within that circle the whole time. Here, we would set up an altar, placing on it forest material and some loose tobacco we had been given as offering. I found a redwood stump that served this purpose well. We could then pray and meditate, or simply hang out and feel a blending into the forest, becoming part of it. I found a place to sit against a stump, feel the earth, and observe. After this time alone, the sound of a drum beaten by one of the assistants would bring us back to the group area in the clearing. There, we would get ready for the second night of journeying, this time with mushrooms.

The mushroom journey had moments of great peace as well as a time of great energy.

During the time of great energy, I felt like I was receiving teaching from an ancient ancestor spirit. Probably more like training than teaching. I don't recall having a vision of the spirit form, as sometimes happens in journeys; but I did feel the spirit's training, manifested as a geometric pattern composed of black and white zig-zag lines. This pattern would appear and then spin, and as it spun, great jolts of energy surged through me. This spinning continued for some time. Occasionally it halted, seemingly to allow me to catch my breath and steady myself, because the surging energy took much psychic or spiritual stamina to sustain without a break. Then, the spinning and the surging energy would repeat. This cycle happened a number of times. I was near exhaustion at the end, but I felt I had been given what I asked for, as unexpected as it was. When I reflected on the experience the next morning, I told the group those old ancestor teachers and healers didn't mess around!

What was the consequence of this spiritual visitation, this training? More opening, more spiritual connection. A stronger connection to spirit, and a greater appreciation and taste of spiritual power and the gift of this teaching, this training.

There were peaceful moments during this mushroom journey, as well. As usual in a group journey, the guide and the assistants occasionally sang to us. One of our guide's memorably moving song had a sweet melody and very simple lyrics: "Love is all there is." Also very moving was one of the assistants' slow and dramatic reading of "Wild Geese." Hearing that song and that poem while on a powerful mushroom journey was breathtaking.

Commentary

Embarking on group journeys outdoors in the forest is a beautiful and deep way to hold ceremony. Whether it was the peaceful ecstasy of the MDMA journey or the world-spinning experience with the ancestor healer, all was welcome and nourishing. The group energy and camaraderie within the redwood wilderness helped us truly become green people.

WILD GEESE

You do not have to be good.
You do not have to walk on your knees
for a hundred miles through the desert, repenting.
You only have to let the soft animal of your body
love what it loves.
Tell me about despair, yours, and I will
        tell you mine.
Meanwhile the world goes on.
Meanwhile the sun and the clear pebbles of the rain
are moving across the landscapes,
over the prairies and the deep trees,
the mountains and the rivers.
Meanwhile the wild geese, high in the clean blue air,
are heading home again.
Whoever you are, no matter how lonely,
the world offers itself to your imagination,
calls to you like the wild geese, harsh and exciting—
over and over announcing your place
in the family of things.

by Mary Oliver

19

MUSHROOM AND 5-MEO-DMT JOURNEY, AUGUST 2021

Intentions

May I help my ancestors heal.
May I open my heart and surrender to the Divine.

Setting

A room in a house in the San Francisco Bay Area; a new location for my guide and me. Daytime. Recorded music, eyeshades, a comfortable mat on the floor, a small altar.

From my guide's notes

[About the pain and suffering of the ancestors] Letting go, let it pass through me.
[During the ancestors' visit] I feel your pain, your pain; you worked so hard; didn't give up. I offer healing for my ancestors. You worked hard so I can be free.

Journey

I began this journey by eating four grams of dried mushrooms in the sacramental manner, and then insufflating about twenty-five mgs of 5-MeO powder in the second phase of the mushroom journey. I consumed a somewhat lower weight of mushrooms this time, but the experience was still powerful. My sensitivity may have been increasing, too, with more experience with or exposure to the medicine.

There were two major phases of this journey.

The first one took place under the mushroom medicine. I asked for a hand-held drum and began to beat it, calling the ancestor spirits who appeared to me in a swarm or cloud. As this visitation began, I expressed gratitude for all their hard work and sacrifices that kept us going, which allowed me to be here.

Then in some mystical way, I experienced much of their pain... hard lives, deaths, murder, war, ravages.... Mostly they were victims, but there must have been perpetrators in there, too. The pain was so awful that I gagged and almost vomited. My guide encouraged me to let the pain pass through me; I did, or at least I did as best as I could. The nausea passed. I believe this visitation allowed some of my ancestors to heal, although perhaps it only scratched the surface. More investigation will undoubtedly follow.

Toward the end of their visit, I assured the ancestors that I would return. I beat the drum as I spoke to them; I told my guide that this would help me connect more easily in the future.

Then it was time for me to insufflate the 5-MeO and move into whatever experience it would provide. As the 5-MeO medicine began to take effect, my guide sprinkled water on me. It felt refreshing after all the work I had been doing. I felt small, cool drops land on my face, and his hands rubbing the liquid on my wrists.

Then the strength of the medicine came on. I was transported to a mystical realm, unimaginable to me beforehand. My consciousness arrived in the presence of the all-powerful Divine. I encountered a power as great as this (egoless) consciousness could possibly take in. I witnessed a golden light, formless—and yet with a sense of enormous weight and mystical structure. I heard a deep, deep vibration, a sound as great as worlds colliding! Pardon the pitifully tiny approximation this description provides. Although I was aware of no body, it was the kind of experience that would make you fall to your knees in deep prostration. In praise of God's glory; in praise of the Divine's power!

I was blessed with this incredible experience for some duration, and then a transition occurred. A faraway spirit appeared in the distance. It gradually approached me, getting closer and closer until it was right before me. The spirit appeared somewhat person-shaped or cross-shaped; and it was composed of a brilliant, electric fire. (See my sketch below, which of course falls short.)

I intuited that this spirit was Christ. Perhaps this was a culturally informed interpretation, but that's how I made sense of the vision. In any case, I believe that this was a teaching face of the Divine. It conveyed a profound truth to me, and with gratitude, I repeat the simple message: Love people, and sacrifice what you need to sacrifice.

Commentary

Although establishing a connection with the ancestors truly was an intense experience, it was dwarfed by my encounters with the Divine and the fiery spirit. And these took on even more significance after I landed from the journey and talked to my guide. I learned that the water he had sprinkled on me and rubbed on my wrists was from the Jordan River in Israel. That seemed notable to me at the time, but I was a little vague on why the Jordan was special. It wasn't until some days later that I remembered that the Jordan was the river where John the Baptist baptized people. I had forgotten this.

I asked my guide why he chose to use this water. He said he had had an intuition of a cleansing opening, clearing and washing away old things, and the Jordan River water seemed to be the right instrument for this. Although I don't think baptism was really on his mind, in fact, I believe that in that moment a kind of baptism by the Divine happened to me.

While reading online about the Jordan, I encountered this quotation from Matthew 3:11: "He will baptize you with the Holy Spirit and fire." My jaw dropped because I understood this scripture from my own experience—the Holy Spirit and fire. Some Biblical scholars fumble over the fire part, interpreting it this way and that. However, in my experience, there was nothing to interpret. It was literally true.

I must report that I am not Jewish or a Christian, although I certainly respect people of all faiths. But spiritual, I am. So, for me, what is baptism? It represents a ritual purification or sanctification. Although I don't say that this journey totally transformed me, it surely was a significant step on my path. And that is enough, really.

I am so grateful for this humbling spiritual experience. Grateful for my guide, these medicines, and the Jordan River water for the door-opening they all provided.

20

Group Mushroom Journey in the Sierra Nevada Foothills, Early March 2022

Intentions

May I connect and talk to the mushroom spirits. Be in relation with them, showing respect and honoring them.
May I connect with an ancestor healer spirit.

Setting

Sierra foothills, Northern California, morning; a large house, fourteen journeyers, three guides. An unusual morning snowfall lent a special purity to the setting. Mats, sleeping bags, eyeshades.

Journey

This morning, I took four and a half grams of dried mushrooms. My journey was quite peaceful overall. I felt chilled near the beginning and asked for a blanket; one of the guides brought it over and caringly tucked all the sides around me. I then went into a deep journey.

In this spiritual space, I encountered two spirits. What type of spirits they were, I know not, although I called on two "types" in my intentions. They were both surrounded by electric fire, like the spirit I had encountered in August the prior year. They had a loving aura, and conveyed the message that there is nothing to fear about bodily death.

Later, I glimpsed the spirits of my parents and grandparents on my mother's side, but I did not dwell there. I felt some deeper ancestral connection, and I may have very well connected to an ancestral healer, but I remain unsure about that.

In the latter part of the journey, when I was back with my ego, still lying on my mat, I heard sad music playing. This elicited grief in me, and quietly my tears came down. I had no idea what I was grieving for, what I had found so sad, but it seems clear to me that this was a quiet grieving. One of the guides noticed and came over and asked if they could sit with me. I said yes. They sat down behind my head and gently stroked my hair. I could feel their loving energy, and myself letting that energy in. This care for me was tender and helped me process this unknown grief. It felt healing for me, too.

Commentary

Even when a marvelous spiritual experience unfolds, it doesn't necessarily translate into many words on paper. Such is the case here. Nevertheless, I feel lucky and blessed to have had this spiritual encounter and teaching.

I grieved towards the end of this journey, a mourning that has been repeated in some other journeys. Grieving about what? A nondescript ocean of pain and suffering? A connection with ancestral suffering? Simply, the suffering of humanity? Whatever it was, it feels totally healthy. It is not easy or pleasant, but I can appreciate the beauty and benefit of this grieving, of honoring the people who came before and their struggles and suffering. Something changes when we grieve, when we feel the loss of someone or something precious, a profound loss of connection.

Here's a saying that emerges: The road to love is paved with grieving.

THE CRYPT

I've opened the door of fear
and stepped inside.
Musty smell, cobwebs, deep dust,
a room long hidden,
a trunk, an old lamp,
books not opened.
Some part of my ancestor's life

If I step into the distant past
will I fall,
be impaled by my fears?
Be eaten by hungry ghosts?

This is so old.
My mother, her mother,
her mother, her mother,
her father, his father,
his father, his father…

Yet the luminescent pearl
starts with grit, broken rock.
Lotus flower rises from mud.
There are ancestors closer to God

Sacred is the wound.
Out of the earth,
the dead are risen

21

Mushroom Journey in the Foothills of the Sierra Nevada, Late March 2022

Intentions

May I connect with and be in respectful relation to helpful loving spirits, be they the mushroom spirit, ancestral healer spirit, or any other supportive spirit.

Setting

Sierra foothills, Northern California. An individual journey in a small house; a different guide than my regular one. Mattress and blanket, eyeshades, an altar.

Journey

I took a 4.6-gram dose of dried mushrooms. Like the group journey earlier that month, this journey had two distinct phases. I visited with spirits in the first part; and the second part produced tears of grieving—a spiritual experience in its own way.

As the journey got underway, a spirit appeared. It was accompanied by a noticeable buzzing sound, like an angry hornet's nest or a deep-noted didgeridoo. I don't recall any visual presentation of this spirit, although there may have been one. But its presence was unmistakable.

Then, a wonderful vision opened. A great crossing between this earthly life and the disembodied spirit world emerged. (See my sketch of souls making the journey and transition—my feeble interpretation of what I experienced.) The transition between worlds or planes of existence has an energetic intensity to it; I sensed it is to be trusted, not feared.

A second spirit subsequently emerged, appearing as a great ball of white light. This visit felt like a communion. Is there a name for this spirit? I could make guesses, but that's all they would be. In any case, the spirt exuded love and wonderment.

The second part of my journey was marked by tears, just like in my previous group journey. This time, however, my grief was considerably bigger and longer. Perhaps some sad music triggered it, but more likely it was just time in the journey for the grieving to begin. Again, there was no particular event or person I recognized as causing the grief; rather I connected to some ocean of ancestral suffering. My guide came over and deeply felt this grief, too. It was in the room with us. In some miraculous harmony, we shared the grief equally, both of us with tears. The experience was loving, connecting, healing, nurturing.

Commentary

Another visitation with spirits, plus an amazing vision! I received a profound vision of the spiritual transition upon the death of the body: it conveyed there is nothing to fear. The subsequent appearance of a new spirit manifested as a ball of light was awe inspiring, filling me with love.

Also truly noteworthy: the field of grief that came over me in the later part of the journey was so big it enveloped my guide as well.

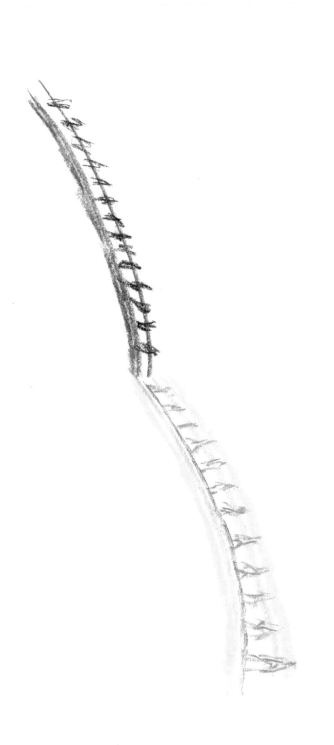

22

Mushroom Journey, Early April 2022

Intentions

May I connect with and be in respectful relation to helpful loving spirits.

Setting

A house in the San Francisco Bay Area. An individual journey with a new guide. A mattress, a blanket, eyeshades, an altar.

From my guide's notes

Spiritual view of dying, how spirit is held and cared for.
Experiencing newness, taking in the soul and it being received in ceremony, then sending it out.
Suffering on this side, not on the other side.

Journey

I took 4.7 grams of dried mushrooms for this journey, which once again was divided into two parts.

The first part was truly intense and spiritual in nature. I witnessed the receiving, caring for, and preparation of a newly released human soul. This was an extended, detailed experience. The soul was brought in and placed on an altar or table. It was orange, and had an orb-shaped appearance. At some point, I felt it was me—my soul—on the altar, getting a firsthand view of the process, perhaps like a preview of what was to come A little of my ego emerged and said, *No I have more to do here, this is not my time*. With this thought, the vision shifted and suddenly I was observing another soul, not my own. The whole experience couldn't have been more powerful, vibrant, or real.

There seemed to be a lead spirit doing the work, accompanied by some other witnessing spirits. These spirits were outlined in a vibrant blue-green hue, ethereal, not filled in. I made a few sketches to share—difficult to capture the experience. The first, more abstract sketch is closer to my actual experience than the more anthropomorphic sketches.

There wasn't a slightest hint of any wrathful deity, making me believe there actually are *no* wrathful deities, contrary to what some traditions teach. I sensed a great peacefulness, along with such loving, gentle care for the soul. Is this what awaits everyone, or only some of us? That's a question I had later, and one I don't have an answer for. Was this a "rehearsal" of my own approaching body death and soul release? I don't have an answer for that, either.

I did not see where the soul was "shipped off" to. That was not part of my experience. Maybe another journey!

The second part of the journey explored suffering. I sensed that great suffering only occurs on this side of the "divide," on this embodied side. Suffering is necessary in some ways (although I don't pretend to know why), and grieving is, of course, necessary, too. The grieving in these journeys has always been about suffering that has happened on earth. However, it is a comfort to know that there is no suffering on the other side, as far as I could tell.

I don't recall any crying during this period of learning, unlike in the prior journeys; just understanding.

As I was drifting down, I reflected more on specific individuals: my mother, currently in the process of dying (I wished her well on her journey); and others in my life.

Commentary

I have had a series of spiritual journeys concerned with the transition from this earthly body and life to what lies beyond. This mushroom journey provided a truly detailed and lengthy view of someone's (my?) spirit being newly received and cared for before moving on to another plane. Big gratitude for this spiritual vision!

Although active grieving was not part of this journey, the journey did explore suffering. The vision highlighted the difference between suffering in this earthly life and its absence in the afterlife—comforting!

23

Mushroom Journey, Late April 2022

Intentions

May I open my heart and surrender to the Divine.
May I connect with and be in respectful relation to helpful loving spirits.
May I explore and experience any grieving that needs to be expressed, whether for my own losses or those of others.

Setting

A small indoor space dedicated to journey work; rural Sonoma County, California. This was an individual journey with a new guide. Although I remained satisfied with my regular guide, I was getting to know how other people worked. As usual, there was a mattress to rest on, along with a blanket and eyeshades. An altar was present.

Journey

The dried mushroom dose was five grams. About halfway through the journey, my guide gave me two 100-mg ketamine lozenges to place under my tongue. The mushrooms were quite strong, and although the ketamine perhaps opened more emotions, the character of the journey remained in mushroom space throughout. I'm told that it is becoming more frequent for guides to mix different medicines in different amounts and at different times in an attempt to enhance experiences. This method was certainly useful for me, keeping in mind that no two journeys are exactly alike.

Once again, the journey was composed of two parts. The first part was characterized by extreme shivering that lasted a long time. I'm not sure why it was so intense; I know the mushrooms were strong, but I don't think they were that different from the ones I had ingested in my recent journeys. Perhaps it had to do with my psychic or spiritual processing. Thinking the shivering would end soon, I kept turning down offers of another blanket; but finally I gave in, and the extra warmth did seem to help—or perhaps it was just time for the shaking to subside. Sometimes, we just don't know!

I felt a great deal of purification taking place. I exerted a lot of energy; it felt like a lot of work. I don't remember much detail beyond that.

In the second part of the journey, I bore profoundly empathic witness to great suffering associated with genocide and brutality. Leading up to this day, I had been spending time with a friend of Spanish descent. His multigeneration-military family traced their lineage all the way back to the conquistadors; and in fact, he claimed that one of his ancestors was a high-ranking officer under Francisco Pizarro, who led the conquest of the Inca Empire. The connection with my friend somehow opened me up to this vision, and I witnessed and wept over the suffering of native peoples as they were brutally slain by these conquistadors. The visions of these brutal murders went on and on. Finally, at some point, I took off my wet eye mask to gaze at a big statue of Buddha, and reflected on how experience and understanding bring forth compassion.

Commentary

Purification and compassion. Those were the two big takeaways from this experience. Compassion, especially, was the capstone, after being flooded with the overwhelming horror of genocide.

I was shocked by these graphic visions of murder, including of women and children. I witnessed what brutality mankind is capable of when I was transported back to this tragic time.

BLUE AND WHITE

Blue and white stripes announce
Greek travelers –
Odysseus and crew
take to their ship

Now to cast off,
raise sail for the
blue horizon,
so perfect, straight, endless

Dark clouds gather,
then up and down
the ship begins to pitch,
gently at first
feeling the swells,
then one slaps the ship hard
and we know we're in it

Getting bigger,
grab the rope
grab the rail
water washes aboard
up my leg, to my chest,
ship shutters and shakes,
pounding hull pounding heart

Wild ride,
can we take more
or will this ship break apart?
Approaching land looks inviting,
but greater danger
those sharp rocks,
and Cyclops holding a giant club

Ah, we sail past the point
and feel the rocking lessen,
journey's end sensed,
praise Athena,
safe at last!

(after a rough journey)

24

GROUP PEYOTE JOURNEY IN THE DESERT, MAY 2022

Intentions

May I open my heart and surrender to the Divine.

Setting

An outdoor group journey, lasting all night long. The Wirikuta high desert, about 6,000 feet in elevation, central Mexico.

Journey

This excursion was led by a curandera, or medicine woman. She was not of the Wixárika people, but she had worked with them with permission for years. Although plenty of Spanish was spoken, the leader and the other bilingual journeyers made sure everyone understood everything said to the group.

The day before, our group had hiked up to the Santuario Wixárika, the shrine on the mountain above the town of Real de

Catorce, to pay homage to the people and their traditions. This land is sacred to the Wixárika (Huichol) people.

This was an all-night fire ceremony, lasting from sunset to sunrise. Our group of twenty people, half from the United States and half from Mexico, had arrived in the afternoon, after piling into the back of an old pickup truck for a very bouncy ride on rough dirt roads, holding on to anything available, bumping into each other, dodging occasional thorny branches. We made camp in an almost entirely treeless area, and formed a circle around the campfire.

After we set up camp, we received instructions on how and where to find the peyote cactus. This slow-growing, small plant, known to many as Grandfather Medicine and locally as hikuri, grows in the partial shade of the area's desert brush. The curandera taught us how to properly harvest the cactus so as not to kill it: don't pick little (young) cacti; cut only the crown; leave a substantial amount of the plant in the ground, cover it lightly with dirt, and give it some water. In time, new buds will appear. We each had a knife for this purpose, and strolled out into the desert alone. It would have been easy to get lost, except that our camp was next to the only tree in sight.

They say you don't find the peyote; it finds you. It took a while for that to happen. I finally spied two cacti growing together. They were kind of old-looking and a bit shriveled, although they were clearly alive when I cut off the crowns—they were wet and green inside. It didn't take too long before a third appeared before me. Although all three were roughly about four centimeters in diameter, this one was younger, healthier. I wished that I'd passed over the first two and found ones that all looked as good as the third, but it wouldn't have been proper not to use what I had already harvested. Having been told that three medium-sized peyote crowns was enough of a dose, I stopped searching and returned to camp with my "buttons."

We set up our spaces for the evening, and cleaned and prepared the peyote for eating. Most of us had brought lightweight camping chairs to sit on. Although it was a warm day in late May, as the sun began to set, the wind picked up and the temperature dropped. We put on whatever layers we had. We were told the evening would be chilly.

The fire ceremony began right after sundown. (See photo.) The ceremony began with prayers and lighting the fire, which was kept burning throughout the night. Then, together, we ate the peyote.

There was a lot of singing that night. Traditional medicine songs led by the curandera, and (surprise!) Hindu songs—led by a Mexican couple who had carried a harmonium all the way out to the desert. All songs and all people were welcome in this congregation of love.

For me, the medicine was not strong, although I could certainly feel it. Younger peyote is said to be more potent, and I suspect that the two older buttons did not have much mescaline. That was somewhat disappointing, but not terribly. It was a pleasure and honor to be with everyone and participate in the nighttime ceremony. There were notable person-to-person encounters, as well as uplifting group energy.

We took a few breaks in the night to hold specific ceremonies. In one of them, the curandera called us up to her one by one, and gave each of us traditional names. Mine was Maxa Juavi, which means Blue Deer in the Wixárika language. I felt honored to receive this name, as the blue deer has a special meaning to the people—it was the spirit guide who led them to peyote. Each journeyer then stood before Grandfather Fire and loudly announced their name so all could hear.

Although I have thrilling and joyful memories of the all-night ceremony, I would be remiss if I didn't also report that this was probably the coldest I have ever been. The temperature didn't reach freezing, but I doubt it was far from it, and the constant wind easily pierced my clothing. We occasionally stood by the fire for some warmth, but it wasn't a place we could stay long. When you add to that no sleeping and no bag to huddle in, it was a trying physical ordeal.

Commentary

I had been waiting for this trip to Mexico and the peyote ceremony with great anticipation. Peyote had been especially important to me when I was younger. In my early twenties, I had several journeys that gave me a sense of spirit, the knowledge that there is something more than this day-to-day physical environment. Although I wouldn't partake in any more psychedelics for another forty-five years, this medicine remained in a special place in my heart.

What a big experience! It required a lot of travel just to reach this part of the world, and the ceremony was physically taxing—but there was a beauty permeating the night and all my fellow travelers. Perhaps it was just as well that the medicine was not very strong for me; I was probably in a better state to absorb all that was happening. No regrets. In fact, it was an honor and privilege to be allowed to participate in ceremony in Wirikuta.

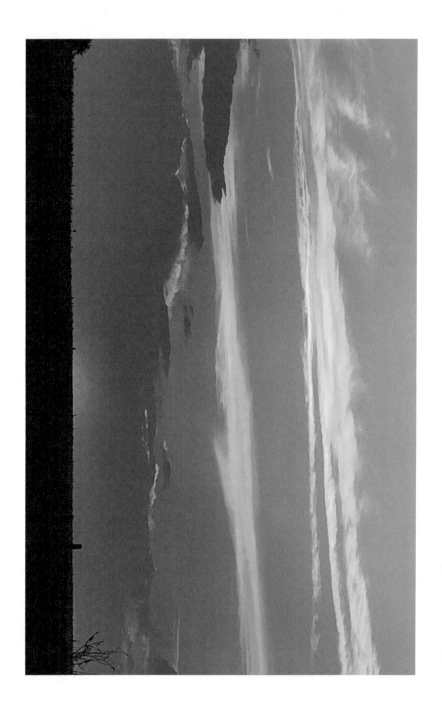

25

Group Morning Glory Journey, Early August 2022

Intentions

May I open to the Divine.

Setting

Mexico; a nighttime journey in a group setting.

Journey

There were eleven of us, all from California and all friends who were familiar with magic mushrooms. Our leader lived in California as well, but he was born and raised in Mexico. He knew the places where we were headed, and he'd made arrangements in advance.

First stop, Mexico City. Saw some sights, especially the wonderful National Museum of Anthropology. From Mexico City, we took a van into the mountains in the state of Oaxaca, up to a town named Hualtla. Hualtla is world famous for magic mushrooms. A healer (curandera) named Maria Sabina of the Mazatec indigenous people lived there decades ago; she was featured in Robert Gordon Wasson's 1957 *LIFE Magazine* article "Seeking the Magic Mushroom." Her story introduced magic mushrooms and the town of Hualtla to the Western world in a big way!

We journeyed with a curandero in the rugged countryside outside of town, in a small structure near his house. (See photo taken near the journey site.) We began in the evening, sitting in chairs in a semicircle around the candle-lit altar. The setting was rustic, to say the least. After a Mazatec-style purification and dedication ceremony, we each were presented with three fresh magic mushrooms wrapped in a large leaf. The mushrooms were large and beautiful. Our focus that night would be on morning glory seeds, but we began by ceremonially eating the mushrooms, which served as a kind of launch pad for the experience.

Next, we were each given twenty morning glory seeds in a folded piece of paper. The seeds were round, about two or three millimeters in diameter, and a light brown color. We ate them slowly, chewing them well and holding them in our mouths for some time before swallowing. There are different varieties of morning glories, and their seeds have different strengths. I don't know which species this was, although I expect they were local.

After eating the seeds, we retired to our mattresses. I put on my eyeshades.

Although the journey was from both medicines and I did feel the mushrooms, I primarily got a sense of these seeds—a soft spaciness; sort of dreamy and pleasant, and fairly strong (of course, strength is always dose-dependent).

My intentions were directed more toward the Divine, but my recollection was that my journey was mostly spent exploring the seeds and reflecting on several relationships.

I asked for more morning glory at some point, to try to get further into that space and learn even more about this seed medicine. The curandero suggested salvia instead, and handed me a wad of wet leaves, roughly one and a half inches across, on a small plate. I took a pinch and chewed as instructed, keeping the leaves in my mouth until they essentially disappeared. This took probably ten or fifteen minutes. The salvia tasted awful, and when my body reacted briefly with a gag, I decided to take no more.

In the morning, the curandero performed a traditional corn reading, throwing about fifteen kernels on a white cloth on the table in front of each of us. As I sat across from him, chickens clucking in the background, the curandero told me, "Que bueno…" Our group leader translated his words from Spanish: "You can obtain God's help in supporting others, and praying to your ancestors to help intercede with God will also help you to bring benefit to others."

Commentary

Although this journey itself was not extraordinary, it was wonderful to be in the land of the Mazatec people, learning a new medicine and new traditions. And my heart was filled traveling with the caring and intriguing people in our group.

¡Que bueno! ¡Con mucho gusto!

26

MDMA and 5-MeO-DMT Journey, Late August 2022

Intentions

May I open my heart and surrender to the Divine.
I ask, please, for teaching, showing, greater understanding, and heart opening.

Setting

An individual journey with my long-time guide in a house in the San Francisco Bay Area. A familiar setting: a floor mattress, eyeshades, a morning start. Peaceful and evocative supportive music playing throughout on the speakers.

From my guide's notes

A lot of reflections.
Feeling love, bliss.

Journey

I began by taking 170 mg of MDMA in a gel capsule, with a planned 70-mg booster about an hour later. This was a pretty strong dose for me, but it had been quite a while since I had journeyed on MDMA and I wanted to go with some gusto. Mission accomplished! The dosage accompanied by the booster worked really well. I experienced a wonderful, blissful feeling with the MDMA, as I reflected on people in my life. It's important to remember that the feel-good properties of MDMA can elicit overly rosy interpretations of your visions, distorting your capacity for realistic assessment and prediction. No harm—as long as you use caution and implement a "cooling-off" period before you take any action following your journey.

After much time with the MDMA, my guide offered me 5-MeO by insufflation, which we had discussed prior to that day. This experience was truly blissful, although in a different way. I asked for a booster, which I had never done before with 5-MeO. I intuited that there was one more level to go, and I did go. Soon after the booster, I totally dissolved into a field of golden light. Non-dual, no ego. A blissful experience of pure spiritual energy.

I came down from the 5-MeO enough for my guide to offer me a snack, but I said not quite yet. I felt really strong energy still in me, like when a rocket takes off and everything is shaking. Interestingly, during the journey when the medicine was even stronger, it was a truly peaceful experience. The 5-MeO is a powerful and profound medicine when used safely and wisely.

Commentary

As the notes show, I spoke very few words. But sometimes, it's not about words or meanings. Sometimes, it's just about the experience. Interesting that during the MDMA portion of my journey, I was able to acknowledge that my interpretations may have been projections of unconscious—or conscious!—desires.

I took a rather large dose of 5-MeO that day, likely about thirty mg or so. My guide did not weigh it out for this journey– instead, he measured it by volume using a tiny spoon. I have grown experienced with this medicine. Dissolving into the golden light is not a simple matter of just having a strong dose. One cannot count on or predict any particular state of consciousness. I accept this experience of spiritual union with deep gratitude. Is this a taste of heaven?

27

Group Mushroom Journey in Sierra Nevada Foothills, September 2022

Intentions

May I connect with spirit guides and healthy ancestors.

Setting

A velada, a traditional Mazatec medicine ceremony, conducted by a curandera visiting from Hualtla, Mexico. A group of friends in the foothills of the Sierra Nevada in California. No recorded music, but prayer and singing. It began around sunset. Eyeshades; mattresses scattered around a large room in a house.

Journey

The curandera began the ceremony outside, smudging each of us individually with the smoke from copal incense and conducting a limpia (cleaning) by touching each of us in a specific pattern with the stem and leaves of a plant. She performed this purification ceremony while praying rapidly. Some of her words were in Spanish and some in the Mazatec language.

We then went inside. We each were given a small paper plate of dried mushrooms with a little honey and three cacao beans. I received four grams. We ate slowly, in ceremonial fashion. Soon, I lay down and put on my eyeshades and pulled up my sleeping bag zipper. Throughout the ceremony, the curandera offered up rapid and repeating prayers, and she and her two assistants sang songs.

As the medicine grew strong, I had chills and some mild shaking for maybe twenty or so minutes. Then, I settled into a very powerful journey.

Soon, I had no awareness of my body or ego. However, I still had observer consciousness. I felt the strong presence of at least two spirit guides or healthy ancestors. I didn't perceive them as embodied, but their spiritual energy was clearly present. They were teaching me, showing and nudging or pulling me toward union with the Divine. I felt movement within an energetic channel toward golden light. Merging, union with God definitely seemed to be the teaching.

Commentary

Sometimes you go to Mexico for a velada, and sometimes the velada comes to California. Although they took somewhat different ritual approaches, both the curandero in Hualtla and the curandera in California conducted ceremonies steeped in

Mazatec tradition. A traditional ritual definitely adds something to the experience. I enjoy and respect it, although I don't believe it's critical to follow that tradition, let alone follow it exactly. I do believe that it is important to bring intentionality and respect to journeys, and to employ ceremony.

The teaching to merge with God was strong. I welcomed that teaching with humble gratitude.

One comment about the words "the Divine" or "God": I often use them interchangeably. The term "God," in particular, holds all sorts of meanings for different people. I don't want to get too far into that, but I do want to say that *I don't know* is a starting point for me. My human brain and the English language can only go so far. I am comfortable interchanging these two words with other words, like "the Universe" or "Buddha Nature." Whatever word or words you prefer, please feel free to substitute.

LINEAGE

My father was Jewish,
of the seed of Abraham.
My mother was Protestant,
followed gospels of Jesus.
But where do I really come from?

Aren't I connected to everything?
Born of Mother Earth,
and what about the
sun and moon,
the stars at night?
That swaying birch branch,
pen contacting paper,
hairs on the arm,
glistening cobweb,
squirrel on the porch.
What a wild family!

28

GROUP MUSHROOM AND 5-MEO-DMT JOURNEY, NOVEMBER 2022

Intentions

Visit with spirit and ancestor guides.
Open to the Divine.

Setting

A group journey beginning after sunset, with seven other participants, my usual, trusted guide, and two assistants. A house in the San Francisco Bay Area. No recorded music, but our guide and his assistants did sing during the ceremony. We wore eyeshades and journeyed on a semicircle of mats on the floor in a large room.

Journey

I ate five grams of dried mushrooms in the ceremonial fashion, taking my time. They felt strong. No chills this time, though. Interesting bluish-greenish patterns arose; and then I moved into the spirit world, hung out there for quite a while. At some point, I thought to ask, *Do you have something to teach me?* And the (non-verbal) answer I received was, "Chill, dude." In other words, just take this in. You don't have to do anything. Just observe and be present. That was the teaching.

After about two hours, the guide gave me a 100-mg lozenge of ketamine. We had discussed using it to possibly enhance the experience. I remember noticing the ketamine's effect, but then I forgot about it. I don't think it had an impact, at least this time. The mushrooms were already quite strong.

Towards the later part of the mushroom journey, I was given a substantial dose of 5-MeO-DMT by insufflation. Quickly, I was transported from this spirit world to a "higher" divine dimension, or at least that's how I make sense of it now. I entered divine light and into the presence of the Divine. This non-dual experience was peaceful and blissful, and lasted a long time. What a gift.

However, as I was landing from the 5-MeO and the mushrooms, there was a sudden shift and a recent conflict came into my consciousness. In a flash, I retched, and my guide brought a bucket for me to spit in. As quickly as the impulse came, it was gone. I felt totally fine. Its energy was purged.

But the episode did raise the memory of an earlier mushroom journey when I also needed to vomit. That time, I experienced a very visceral vision of my own childhood murder, along with my parents', at the hands of Nazi soldiers.

Very quickly, that memory expanded to encompass grief for the thousands and millions of children in this world who have been murdered. I asked for a ceremonial rattle, which an assistant brought to me. I shook it loudly. There was silence in the room, reverence for the great sound of this rattle penetrating the candle-lit space. I said out loud to all present, "I shake this rattle for all the murdered children." I then wept tears of deep grief. When those were finished, I lay on my back to rest.

Commentary

One can never predict how a journey will go. There's no point in even trying.

In this group journey, under a strong dose of magic mushrooms, the spirits came forth with a simple, wise, and perhaps humorous teaching: "Chill." Just observe. Just hang out with us. Be patient with the spiritual plane.

Okay! I can do that.

With the aid of the 5-MeO, a "higher" (I presume) plane or essence was revealed, one that I've been blessed to experience before. Namely, a blissful merging with divine light. Such an experience isn't just about blissing out, however. It's a gift, a blessing that's perhaps more about understanding than feeling, although both are so impactful. The understanding and the feeling are about the experience, however, and not cognition.

MAGIC

What is this magic called life?
Who ordered it up? Made it happen?
Created sweet and bitter?
Gave us a second chance?
And a third and fourth?
Thank you, thank you.
Whatever, whoever, however

29

Group Ayahuasca Journey, December 2022

Intentions

Learn more about ayahuasca, the Grandmother medicine.
Visit and learn from helping spirts, healthy ancestor spirits.

Setting

A two-night group retreat in a large house in rural Sonoma County, California. Mats were spread around the perimeter of a large room. I was one of ten participants; we had two guides who specialize in working with ayahuasca, aka the Grandmother Medicine.

Journey

Usually, ayahuasca ceremonies are held in groups of various sizes. (A ten-journeyer group is pretty modest.) I had had my first experience with ayahuasca during the height of COVID, in an individual journey with a guide. I wanted to experience it again, this time in the more traditional group setting. Admittedly we were in California, not the Amazon; however, both guides had spent some years in the Amazon basin.

The two guides sat on either side of an altar propped against the center wall. A small plastic purge bowl was provided for each of us. The journeys began after sunset. There was no recorded music, but the two guides sang medicine songs, some in English and some Peruvian icaros.

There were bedrooms in the large house where we could sleep after the medicine had subsided, and a big breakfast was served following the two nighttime ceremonies.

After settling in, introducing ourselves, and reviewing the plan for the evening, we were invited to go outside and begin the ceremony with a tobacco cleansing. This took place soon after sunset. We used mapacho tobacco, a strong South American varietal, steeped in water to create a light, brown-colored liquid. Our guides poured a little water into each of our cupped hands; we then quickly brought the liquid into our noses, tilting our heads back and quickly inhaling in one motion. The result? Tobacco water, or some of it, anyway, found its way well into our sinuses. Talk about a wake-up!

Is this really a cleansing? Hmmm. As the reader may guess, I'm not convinced. It certainly opens the sinuses in a stimulating way.

Ayahuasceros have a sort of love affair with tobacco. Snuff and smoking tobacco play significant roles in this tradition, along with the mapacho cleansing method. I smoked cigarettes for much of my twenties and had a heck of a time quitting. So glad I finally did. Maybe that colors my perspective. Could be. Suffice it to say, I'm not impressed by or enamored with the use of tobacco, whether it be mapacho or any other variety. But I digress. And this tobacco juice cleansing was only a small part of the evening, although it marked the beginning of the ritual.

Ayahuasca is a dark brown, viscous liquid brewed from two or more plants. We were told this batch came from Hawaii and was made solely from the two principal plants, with no other constituents. That's a good thing, I believe. Ayahuasca is known as a purgative. It often induces vomiting, a while after ingestion. Some say that's also a good thing, that it cleanses the spirit and/or psyche. For me, the jury is also still out on that score.

Back to the ceremony. One at a time, we came up to the guide, who poured the liquid into a small plastic cup. This brew was easy to drink; it had a little sweetness to it. You could ask for more or less of a standard volume of the liquid. (You could also ask for more when offered an hour or so later.) We drank the ayahuasca right then and there, before returning to our mats. For the first night's ceremony, I received what was said to be a standard volume.

The beginning of this journey was marked by modest visuals—colors and patterns—which then faded. I felt spirit and ancestor support, and I reflected on "stuff."

The second night, I asked for a larger amount so I could further explore this medicine. It was about 50% more than the first night. Again, as we all did, I drank it down as it was handed to me.

This was definitely a stronger journey. My intentions were unchanged, and this time, the spirits appeared forcefully, right in front of me. You could say up close and personal. The message they gave was that I was still holding some fear and I needed to be rid of it. Immediately, I needed to reach for the plastic purge bowl, and I dry heaved into it, one time. It felt like I was expelling fear. With that, I felt relief and lay back down onto my mat. I don't recall much of the rest of the journey other than it was peaceful.

Commentary

On journeys with magic mushrooms or 5-MeO, a sudden wave of nausea occasionally appears. Not sure there was anything specific to the ayahuasca that contributed in this regard, although there might have been. Ayahuasca admittedly is tough on the digestive tract, but this felt more like an energetic release than an upset stomach.

I have enjoyed my group experiences, and this one was no different. A loving, accepting spirit permeated the atmosphere. Although tobacco is not my thing, I enjoyed the ceremonial aspects of the journey, especially the guides singing traditional medicine songs.

The strong appearance of spirits the second night was welcome, as was the release of fear. I don't know if the fear was of anything in particular. Perhaps fear of death? Not sure. But I am grateful for the lesson and release. I can't say there is no fear left, but I felt lighter afterward.

GRANDMOTHER

Grandmother is an elder.
She possesses wisdom and is willing to share.
What can we say to honor her?

She carried life for countless generations,
blood and water flow through her still.
She can be rough if she needs to
or gently embrace.
She herself flows like a river,
like the Amazon,
deep and wide,
teeming with life.
Some scary creatures
live in that water
and beautiful creatures too.
An abundance of life-giving water
to drink, cook and wash.

Grandmother sees so much!
Gratitude for Grandmother!

30

Group LSD Journey, February 2023

Intentions

Learn more about LSD as a medicine.
Visit with helping spirts, healthy ancestor spirits.

Setting

A small group journey in a little house in rural Sonoma County, California. I was one of four participants.

Journey

There were two guides and one assistant guide, all familiar with working with LSD. The high ratio of guides to journeyers was reflective of the length of the journey; simply, it is a lot of work and a long day to be a guide for LSD participants. LSD journeys can take as long as twelve hours, and this one was no exception—we began in the morning and ended in the evening. We journeyed on two mats and two couches in the living room; I was on one of the mats. Afterwards, we gathered together for a group dinner and then slept over at the house. The next morning, we met for an integration session and returned home.

We each were given about 0.75 grams of dried mushrooms as a starting point for the trip. Not sure that mattered, but it was a comfortable beginning. Then, we took our doses of LSD. Using an eyedropper, our guide squeezed a drop of solution on top of our hands, placing it in the crease between the thumb and index finger of a gently held fist so it wouldn't roll off. We licked the solution—exact dose unsure, but probably one hundred micrograms or more. I wore my eyeshades in the beginning, although I took them off some hours later.

This journey started off with a bang!

It was as though I was thrown into the middle of Carnival in Rio de Janeiro, only instead of being shoulder to shoulder with vibrant dancers, there were spirits EVERYWHERE! If I had a jaw, it would have dropped! Absolutely awe-inspiring and shocking—in a wonderful way. It felt like a gift from the spirit world, inviting me to their festival, their Carnival. I don't remember communicating with the spirits, just being among them, witnessing how many there were. I don't really know what kind of spirits they were; maybe I'll find out some other time.

Afterwards, it occurred to me that my experience made laughable the question… are there spirits? I sketched a simple drawing trying to capture the experience. This adventure was certainly the highlight of this journey.

And it was a long, long journey. There was time for other parts. Sometime later, I went outside and sat on the deck with one of the guides. I remember paying homage to Bubbe and Zayde, my father's parents, acknowledging their suffering and sacrifice in coming to the United States around 1900, undoubtedly to escape the Russian pogroms. This led me to reflect upon and express gratitude to all my ancestors for their sacrifices bringing me to this present moment.

Somewhat later still, I wondered whether I was coming down from the medicine. I realized that that was just not happening yet. It already had been a long trip, many hours—and many, many calories expended by my brain. I could sense how frustrating it would be to have a serious mental illness where your brain didn't function properly. I wasn't worried about that for myself, just aware that this would be a long journey, and I would be coming down at some point! And yes, I did come down in due course.

Commentary

If you had to sum up psychedelic journeys in a word, "unexpected" would be a good one.

Although I had had visits with spirits before, the sheer number of them this time was astounding, and opened up a new perspective for me. And why not? Why would there only be a spirit here and there? After all, there are billions of humans on this planet, so it makes total sense that there are multitudes of spirits—but to witness them was something else.

You may ask the question... is there something about LSD that is truly different than magic mushrooms or ayahuasca? Does it open a bigger door or let you go deeper? I don't think so. I think this spirit-filled journey was just a natural next step. These medicines are door openers; they are not what is on the other side of the door. Maybe sometimes they open different doors? Maybe the same medicine sometimes opens a different door? Anyway, as I get more experience with LSD, I expect to learn more about it and its differences from other medicines. So much is a mystery.

The next morning, in integration circle, I described my experience with the spirit Carnival. One guide looked at the other and commented that they had just received a postcard from a friend depicting a big Carnival parade in Nice, France. Of course, I knew nothing about the postcard before that. How about that?!

DANCE OF THE SPIRITS

You don't see them at breakfast,
or at the grocery store,
so are they even real?

Suddenly the world opens up
and all around are spirits!
Alive, moving, welcoming

Here's the spirit world!
Suddenly, like a wide boulevard in
Rio at Carnival,
dancing and prancing

31

GROUP HUACHUMA JOURNEY, MAY 2023

Intentions

May I open to the Divine.

Setting

A temple next to a house in rural Northern California. A group journey with five participants, a guide, and an assistant guide. Backjacks (floor chairs), tri-fold twin mattresses, and yoga mats were provided. We all brought objects for an altar that we set up in the middle of the floor.

Journey

Note: huachuma, also known as San Pedro, is the name for a cactus native to the Andes Mountains. Like peyote, huachuma contains mescaline; unlike peyote, it grows quickly and large.

Medicine from mescaline-containing cacti is known as Grandfather Medicine.

Although my group journey with peyote in Mexico, back in May 2022, was positive, the dose was weaker than I had hoped for. I was looking for something stronger, to harken back to what I remembered from my experiences with peyote when I was in my twenties.

We slept over on Friday and Saturday nights; the journey started on Saturday morning, around 9 AM. This medicine is good for daytime use—eyes open and time spent outside—and it provides a long journey, easily lasting ten hours.

Our guide specialized in the huachuma medicine; he knew it well. At the start of the ceremony, he asked us individually what size dose we wanted. I requested a full, strong dose, also knowing that a second serving would be available in an hour and a half. He gave me about twelve ounces of the dark brown, slightly viscous liquid. He also provided pieces of ginger to suck or bite on, to make drinking the liquid easier. Huachuma is not easy to swallow, but by taking multiple small sips alongside the ginger, it was doable.

We waited until everyone was served so we could drink the medicine together. Our guide invited us to do gentle yoga poses after drinking. This got our bodies working, and by about the time the yoga stopped, around thirty minutes later, I could feel the medicine's energy rising.

This time, my journey was strong and very beautiful, not overpowering, but with a bright, spiritual quality. I lay back on the mattress, thinking, "Finally!" This was what I had been waiting for.

I felt a sense of gratitude and relief as the journey began. The guide turned on some gentle recorded music, and he occasionally sang and played the harmonium.

We were allowed to go outside and walk or sit or lay down, but for the first hour or two, I stayed inside, lying down on my mat, absorbed by the energy, feeling wonderful. I soon had a sense that a major theme of this journey would be purification.

I prayed, "Please purify me." Not that purification hadn't been happening (it had), or that it won't continue (it probably will). But a distinct sense of being purified flowed through me.

I went outside at some point and lay on the ground, feeling the earth beneath me and sunshine above me. Blissful, with a sense of tranquility.

I could perceive the Divine throughout the journey, a grandeur, a brightness, a luminescence. Absorbing the bigness of the spiritual energy, with gratitude.

Appreciation for this Grandfather Medicine, and appreciating that I am a grandfather, too.

Perhaps ten or more hours after the start, our guide held a lovely limpia (cleaning) ceremony to close the formal part of the journey. He held a bouquet of bay leaves in each hand and sang a cleaning song as he playfully and ceremonially patted us down. The lyrics spoke of paddling a canoe down the river to the sea.

All in all, a beautiful day! Followed by a healthy and tasty hot dinner in the main house, and a warm shower. Many thanks,

Grandfather Medicine! And thanks to our guide, his assistant, and my fellow travelers!

Commentary

Closure? Or maybe a better word is connection. I feel like this huachuma journey connected me with my youthful experimentation and insights with peyote. There was something deeply satisfying about that aspect.

However, the big picture was just that—the big picture. The brightness of the Divine and the purification provided. This experience stands on its own as big and beautiful, meaningful and majestic.

I am deeply grateful.

Photo is of El Capitan in Yosemite National Park. This massive rock evokes Grandfather Spirit for me.

32

GROUP MUSHROOM JOURNEY IN MEXICO, SEPTEMBER 2023

Intentions

May I connect to the spirits of this land.
May I connect to ancestors.

Setting

A retreat center near the small town of San Jose del Pacifico; 8,000 feet altitude in the Sierra Madre del Sur, in the Mexican state of Oaxaca.

Journey

Full cycle. The beginning of a new cycle.

San Jose del Pacifico is where my traveling friend and I obtained mushrooms in the summer of 1972.

This was a big journey, a big life event for me.

The adventure began in the city of Oaxaca. Our guide and organizer was a lovely medicine woman from Colorado.

Together with her Mexican assistant and seven other participants, we enjoyed two pleasant days in the city.

Especially noteworthy was the late-evening walking tour, led by a young, newly minted human rights attorney. He told us he was 100% Zapotec, a major indigenous group in that area of Mesoamerica. Spanish was his mother tongue, and he spoke very good English. He only spoke a few words of Zapotec; he said he intends to learn it, but it's a difficult language, with subtle tonality.

Our guide shared his family history with us, explaining why he did not grow up speaking Zapotec. His great-grandfather died when his grandfather was young. When he was eight years old, his grandfather went to the nearby river to fetch water. There, he was kidnapped by Spanish men who took him to town and enslaved him. He led a terrible life as a young man, often sleeping outside like a dog and working constantly. He knew no Spanish when he was enslaved; and the first phrase he learned was, "What do you want me to do?"

When he was about eighteen years old, our guide's grandfather escaped his captors and made his way back to his village in the jungle.

And now, why was our guide not taught Zapotec? Because his grandfather associated being Zapotec with being unsafe, subject to being enslaved, and he didn't want anything to do with it. Better to assimilate, he thought.

A terrible tragedy.

I repeat this story as it is so central to the world here, and because it connects to an incident which was to follow.

Our walking tour continued, and we stopped near the Basilica de Nuestra Señora de la Soledad. There, our guide told us two different stories of how the church came to be. One was the Catholic version: someone had a vision of the Virgin Mary at that location. Another was the Zapotec story: this was a sacred site where people came to listen for the sound of an underground stream. After he told us these two stories, our guide asked us, "Which do you choose to believe?"

He pointed at the Basilica, asking, "Why such high stone walls?" The answer was that the cathedral was also a fortress, to protect the Spanish colonists from unhappy indigenous people.

He told us about tunnels leading from the church to the nearby convent, which he believed were built for emergency escape. In the early twentieth century, workers discovered babies' bodies hidden behind the walls of the tunnels. The priests and nuns lived together in early times, and when a baby appeared... it was killed. Most of the little bones were found in boxes. Our storyteller inferred it would have been too uncomfortable for a priest to directly kill the baby, so they were placed in little coffins to die. He also told us that sometimes a nun would escape the convent and then be captured, presumably because she knew too much. The space was too small for an intact adult body, but the workers excavating the tunnel walls found sections of adult skeletons.

I was aware of atrocities brought upon the indigenous people of this land by the Spanish and the Catholic Church. Large scale rape and genocide; the extinguishing of long-held customs. Indeed, I witnessed some of these atrocities in my mushroom journey in April 2022. The stories our guide told added to my understanding.

The next day, our group piled into a van and took the several-hour drive on a winding road to San Jose del Pacifico. We stayed in pleasant rustic cabins at a retreat center. Pleasant— especially when there was hot water for showers (not always available). Our experience in the mountains lasted two and a half days. It was conducted by a family led by a woman curandera, her medicine man husband, and three middle-age children. The family lived in a simple compound on the outskirts of town. They worked as a cohesive unit, and their intent was clearly and carefully therapeutic, as well as spiritual. They all were loving and beautiful beings.

There were no visible crosses or images of Our Lady of Guadalupe at their site, and while respect was shown to Christians, the common words of homage spoken in ceremony was to our Mother Earth. I did not once hear the words "Jesus Cristo." This was quite different than my experience in Hualtla. It was clear that this family was connected to their pre-Columbian traditions and considered Catholic conversion to be wrong for them. In fact, the father told us that his many siblings believed he was working for the devil, and sadly, no longer spoke to him.

We spent the afternoon of the first day going one by one for a private "diagnosis" with the curandera. We each were accompanied by one of the two group members who were fluent in Spanish—our leader and her assistant, a man from Mexico. The diagnosis began with a limpia (cleaning, purification) using a handful of wet herbs. The curandera brushed me down with the herbs and lightly slapped them against me a few times, all the while praying and chanting.

Then, the diagnosis itself. The curandera rubbed a raw egg over me, again while praying. She broke the shell and let the egg fall into a glass of water. The top half of my glass mostly remained full of clear water; just a wisp of egg white rose to the surface. She read that as strong spirit. The yolk was solid, well contained, and she told me that meant that my body was in a healthy and well-toned condition. She added that I was close to completing an undertaking, which I can interpret in multiple ways in my personal life, including returning to these mountains and finishing this book. The egg white mostly sank to the bottom of the glass, and she said that signified sadness. This didn't surprise me, given my own and my ancestors' history.

I was given an opportunity to ask questions. I asked what she thought about my returning to San Jose del Pacifico after fifty-one years. The curandera replied that this return represented the start of a new cycle.

We concluded the day with a nourishing and tasty meal.

The next morning, we returned from our lodgings to their compound. First, we did some wild dancing, accompanied by two drums. One of the sons led the dancing, shell cuffs rattling around his ankles, while his sister and our Mexican group assistant played a loud surging rhythm on the drums. There were different dances, one right after the other. It was a workout!

We paired up for one of the dances and were instructed to keep tight eye contact with our partner. Every few minutes, we moved on to the next person and repeated this dance until we had danced with nearly everyone. I love and value these eye-contact practices. This one was a treat, with its wild, rhythmic dancing and deep bonding. Most of my partners looked at me closely, but a couple could manage only occasional eye contact. The curandera was one of my partners. Her eyes practically bulged with intensity, which was wonderful.

Our afternoon activity, clay therapy (reminiscent of sandbox therapy), was inspired by modern psychotherapy. I was surprised but welcomed it. We sat on cushions in a large circle on the open wooden floor. We each had a lump of maybe two pounds of clay in a wooden frame. The curandera sat in a chair next to her daughter, a professional psychotherapist who led the activity.

She directed us to think of something meaningful from our egg drop diagnosis or our life, and to craft our clay to represent that. All the other group members made something accordingly. Nothing came to me, so I began by repeatedly pressing my two thumbs into the clay, into the earth. At some point, looking down at how the clay was being transformed, I realized, "Oh, it's a tree." I then made some small adjustments, notably adding a trunk, but otherwise the composition essentially was already finished.

After we completed this task, we took turns sharing and the psychotherapy began. (The therapist spoke in Spanish and one of our two translating members assisted.) Often with perceptive questions and comments, she led each of our group members into our psychic woundings, caringly but with authority, occasionally quietly conferring with her curandera mother. New insights were common in the group, as were tears.

For myself, I explained how my clay picture of a tree emerged without forethought. The therapist asked what I thought it meant. I replied, "The tree of life." She asked about my family, and I replied that I had two grown children and three grandchildren. I added that I appreciate and am at peace with my position as an elder. She asked how my heart is ("¿Cómo está tu corazón?"), and I replied, "Está bien" (It is well). That was my turn with the clay.

That evening, we had temescal, a kind of sweat lodge. This is a traditional purification ritual held in a dome-shaped stone structure. It was tight quarters! We all sat on woven mats on the ground, circling a pit. An assistant shoveled large, red-hot stones through the sole small entrance, and the elder man then arranged them in the pit. The elders sat on either side of the entrance. The medicine man led this ceremony, periodically tossing water onto the stones and making steam. Most of the time, a heavy canvas cloth covered the entrance.

There were four parts to the ceremony. At the beginning of each part, as the shovelfuls of hot stones were delivered, we all shouted, "¡Da!" which meant, "Welcome, stones!"

I won't get into too much detail on the structure of the ceremony, but there was a part connecting to childhood through childhood songs, and a part connecting with ancestors. There was a good deal of singing. To my surprise, the group members sang quite a lot of pop songs, which I had not previously encountered in the many ceremonies I'd attended. I wasn't particularly thrilled by this, but one of the things I learned during my experience in San Jose del Pacifico was for me to loosen up. Okay! Pop songs in ceremony! (I'm still not *advocating* pop songs in ceremony, though.)

It was a difficult experience, long (one comrade reported two and a half hours), and at times extremely hot. We were each given a rattle to use when directed to, along with a bunch of marigolds that we were to hold in front of our faces during the hottest moments. They felt essential, as I had never experienced such intense heat in my prior temescals. Afterwards, everyone, even those decades younger than me, said they were pushed to the limit of their endurance. I was the oldest member, and although in reasonably good condition, I was certainly at my limit.

When it was finally time to emerge from the cramped stone structure, we crawled out of the small opening and quickly went to a pool of cold water, scooping it out using half-coconut shells and shouting as we poured the water over our heads.

Upon reflection, my sense is that there was no need, and no apparent benefit, to making this temescal so difficult. Do I know that for certain? No. But I trust my sense about it. Although there was still value in it, this temescal felt out of balance.

The next morning was the mushroom ceremony. We were surprised to wake up to no running water. How; why? We never found out. Later, I wondered whether this inconvenience was an intentional part of our preparation—but I was assured it was not. Nevertheless, with a minimum of sleep and no water to wash or even to flush a toilet, we began the day with a sense of moving forward however we needed to.

Now to the central experience of this trip to the mountains, our ceremony with Teonanácatl, which in the Nahuatl language literally means "god mushroom."

After the short transport back to the curanderos' compound, we were greeted with small cups of hot chocolate. The ten of us then were driven some distance into the rugged mountain countryside, making our way down a winding dirt road until we came to a clearing owned by the family.

This was an outdoor group mushroom journey, in a fifty-by-one-hundred-meter clearing with a few pine trees and a pine needle forest floor. Most of us took off our shoes to better feel Mother Earth. We began in late morning. The mountain clouds floated above. The mountain air was crisp but not unpleasant. As we sat down together in a circle, I noticed a small ground plant waving to me. It was happy to see me.

The medicine man began by singing ritual songs and led us in one or two simple songs, I assume in the Zapatec tongue. (It clearly wasn't Spanish.)

Next, the curandera opened two bags of varied colored rose petals and instructed us to create an image for an altar. She said that based on the group's diagnoses and clay therapy, the most appropriate image was a uterus and ovaries. She showed us a picture on her smartphone to help us get started. Together, we created a beautiful image, about a meter across. I stepped away briefly when it was essentially complete. When I walked back, a mug was sitting on the rose-petal altar. For some unknown reason, I picked up the mug to remove it; I suppose I sensed that it didn't belong. I was immediately told with some alarm that I was removing an offering and to put it back, which I quickly did. More on this incident later.

Then they gave us our mushrooms, one by one, held in a large leaf. I believe the amount differed for different members, but they were substantial for each of us. There were two types of fresh mushrooms served, derrumbe (landslide) and pajaritos (little birds). I had two of the larger derrumbe mushrooms and a large number of the smaller pajaritos.

After eating our mushrooms, drinking a mushroom tea, and, if we wished, eating honey with more mushrooms, we all scattered around the clearing. I had a small camping blanket to lie on. No eyeshades, but I ended up keeping my eyes closed for most of the journey. I settled under a tree and began my journey sitting. As the medicine gathered strength, I lay down, closing my eyes.

My psychedelic journey began with being transported to the spirit world. It appeared almost like a town or city. It took some energy to stay with it, but I did for some time. I had no sense of self, just simple awareness. I felt spirits present, but didn't interact with them at first.

After some time, I sought and found paternal ancestors, including my father and my recently deceased oldest brother observing nearby. This was a peaceful encounter. I felt their acceptance of and respect for my medicine work. I told them I would join them before long.

That concluded my time spent in the spirit world. In my journey space, I then visited with friends and family who are still living. This also was peaceful, pleasant.

At some point, I heard the whole medicine family approach me. They were visiting each of us journeyers, one by one. They came with copal incense, chimes, and beautiful singing, encircling me as I sat up. There were probably six or so of them, including the two elders. I am grateful for their loving and supportive gift. It was one of the most beautiful ceremonial moments ever provided to me.

During the later part of my journey, I suddenly understood why I had removed the mug from the flower-petal altar. The mug contained chocolate, representing life and death. My act played a role in a teaching, and I was an instrument of the teaching. What was the lesson? Colonization. The taking away of what belongs to others. When I removed the mug, I was re-enacting a form of colonialism. This teaching fit with our whole experience in southern Mexico: our late-night walking tour of Oaxaca, discussing the trauma-filled history of the Basilica, learning why our curanderos let go of Catholicism... It all culminated in that mug of chocolate.

There is mindless and mindful colonization. My act was mindless. I wasn't thinking about what I was doing. A lot of colonization is mindless—people taking what is not theirs and harming others because they have been taught to believe it is the right thing to do. The immigrant Spanish priests truly believed the indigenous people were primitives who worshipped the devil and needed conversion (or death). Similarly, the Spanish colonists truly believed they were carrying out their king's divinely appointed mandate to appropriate the indigenous people's land. In addition, there was—and still is! —mindful, that is, deliberate colonization. People already sitting at the top of the power pyramid knowing full well what they are doing, often operating out of greed, hatred, and fear. This whole experience in Mexico took place where the terrible stain of colonization persists.

Commentary

This was BIG. Some other words that come to mind are closure, completion, renewal. Returning to San Jose del Pacifico after fifty-one years for a powerful and beautiful mushroom ceremony in the mountains was a blessing. My whole experience in southern Mexico was profound, part of my lifelong journey of learning, healing, and growth. I am deeply grateful to the people of this land, my group comrades, and the beautiful medicine family who hosted and guided us.

Photo taken in San Jose del Pacifico

33

Group 5-MeO-DMT Journey, October 2023

Intentions

May I explore the unknown and connect to spirit.

Setting

San Francisco Bay Area, a house in the woods. A group journey with six participants, including me, and three guides.

Journey

This was a Friday-to-Sunday retreat centered on experiencing a new way of serving the 5-MeO medicine, namely by inhaling it through a vape pen. By now, I was pretty familiar with insufflating this medicine, and I was interested in learning a new way of administration. Of course, there are pros and cons to all approaches; the vape pen provides simplicity as well as quite a bit of flexibility, especially since different pens hold different concentrations. The length of duration of the full effect is rather short, like ten to fifteen minutes; this can be a drawback, although it offers flexibility, a plus. There is also a drifting down time that can be useful for both methods.

We first got familiar with the logistics of the approach and the sensation of the medicine at modest doses. This was done as a group and made for some nice bonding.

Next, we had an opportunity, if we wished, to explore larger doses with a more concentrated pen, starting with a lower concentrated pen as a gentle onramp. We separated into three groups, each with a guide and two participants. Taking turns, the journeyer lay on a mattress with the guide and the other participant assisting as need be. There were two rounds of this—one on Saturday and one on Sunday.

The first time, as I entered the higher strength of the medicine with my eyes closed, the light became bright, accompanied by a strong body sensation that's a bit difficult to describe. It gave a powerful opening and blissful feeling—provided you surrender to its effect, which I did. As this medicine works its magic at this higher dose, you most definitely encounter the Divine, or "touch spirit" as one of the guides liked to say. Truly a gift. In fact, some people call this the God molecule.

It takes a significant amount of time to drift down from this peak as the medicine subsides, and we were told this can be a valuable space for therapeutic work. Indeed, I spontaneously began to reflect on an approaching visit to my sister-in-law dying of cancer, an opportunity to visit and say good-bye. The grief of losing her suddenly washed over me and I was able to mourn in a gentle and healthy way. The guide offered her hand over my heart, which I accepted—comforting and helpful for the grieving to flow. Therapeutic, to be sure.

On Sunday, we had another opportunity to take 5-MeO by vape, partnering with another one of the guides and participants. Again starting with a lower concentration pen and then moving to the higher concentration one, I entered a powerful state, experiencing the Divine energy. I relaxed into the blissful field of light. We had spoken beforehand about the guide (a young woman) possibly placing her hand over my heart as I climbed to the height of the journey; I had said yes; and this she did. Her hand was gentle, comforting.

As I began to drift down from this height, another therapeutic opportunity spontaneously presented itself—this time in a much more surprising way. Perhaps her feminine hand over my heart while I was in this medicine was the catalyst. In any case, I began to explore my own abandonment as an infant, and I realized that I wasn't abandoned now. I began to say gently to myself, "I'm not abandoned now." And although those words are simple, there suddenly was a definite shift in my own spirit, my own psyche, and a release of the lifelong grief I have been carrying from this great wounding. Unlike the day before, this wasn't a grieving but rather a release of held grief, held sadness.

This is not to say there hasn't been healing of this wound along the way—there has. Some chapters clearly speak to it. I can't say for certain this was the final step of healing, either, but it did feel that way. Most welcome and profound! So surprising.

Commentary

In the previous chapter, I describe a major completion of a cycle—my experience with magic mushrooms when I was a young man, and my recent return trip to re-explore Mexico and these medicines. A real life cycle. And as the curandera told me, a new cycle was starting.

Before this retreat, I had described my time in Mexico using the words "closure, completion, renewal." And while those words did apply to what transpired in Oaxaca, they also foreshadowed what was to come here in California.

What set this great wheel in motion was my early experience of abandonment and my internalization of that trauma, with its associated pain and grief. With this surprise healing of my early wound, an even greater cycle has been completed.

Perhaps I have truly come full circle, now. I wonder what will come next. In any case, I sense that this is a proper place to close this book.

Epilogue

Thank you for reading my story, for accompanying me on my path with psychedelics. A winding path, to be sure. Or, if you prefer, a meandering river, with occasional rapids, full of life and learning.

There has been suffering and joy, astonishment, grief, and grace. Much healing and growth, and consequently, change in me—I can even say *transformation.*

For me, healing from my sacred wounds is not really distinct from spiritual growth. I won't say these two are identical, but there is much overlap.

Where did my path begin? Good question. With my birth in 1951? In the distant past, a thousand generations ago? I reported witnessing what I believe to be a past life; and where there's one, there are certainly many more. But let's start with this present embodiment.

Fair to say, my path began in infancy and early childhood with abandonment and emotional neglect—a deep psychic wounding. Separation is the source of emotional and spiritual pain. That pain for me was inflamed by the internal struggle between wanting connection and fearing connection—manifested by a self-reliant protection strategy. I was walking around carrying this struggle, unconsciously, of course. No wonder I was self-medicating with wine every evening, as well as displaying other less-obvious symptoms of distress.

Thank goodness for the opportunity psychedelic-assisted therapy provided me. I feel fortunate, indeed.

And yet, the landscape of this path has been much larger than just my personal story. It has been transpersonal, other worldly. There has been connection with the Divine; there have been contacts with the spirit world. Profound grief flooded my consciousness on numerous occasions. Sometimes this grief was about immediate family members; but more so, it came from an ancient and larger ground.

Walking this path has been a constant moving forward, like the motion of my horse spirit animal. That means leaving behind old wounds and things that no longer serve. These powerful medicines provide psychic and spiritual release, sometimes manifested by a deep crying, a shout of anger, a sudden physical retch—they can be an energetic purgative. Sometimes, these medicines act more as door openers, unlocking our hearts and emotions, or connecting us to the Divine.

It bears repeating that all of my journeys were taken in the presence of one or more guides. Many people have written about why guided journeys are recommended over journeying on your own. It's not that something good *can't* happen without a qualified guide-therapist, but there are reasons to work with a well-trained guide. Injury happens in relation to people (or, in their absence—neglect, abandonment), so it makes sense that healing happens in relation to people, as well. Being with someone you trust and feel safe with while in an altered state of consciousness allows space for your psyche and spirit to relax and open. And although arising material still can be quite challenging, a knowledgeable, supportive guide can help journeyers avoid traumatizing "bad trips."

Many of my journeys took place in group settings. There is a beauty and helpful collective energy that community provides. And some of my journeys were in nature—in community with Mother Earth.

With gratitude, I honor the healing strength of these powerful medicines and the wisdom of our ancestors who have brought these ways to us.

I wish everyone a journey full of love.

About the Author

Chris Becker is a scientist and an inventor as well as a writer. He holds a Ph.D. in chemistry from the University of California, Berkeley, and is author on many peer-reviewed scientific journal articles and U.S. patents. He published his first book *Healing with Psychedelics: Essays and Poems on Spirituality and Transformation* in 2020. Straddling science and spirituality, Chris has also practiced Buddhist meditation before and during the walking of this path. He lives in the San Francisco Bay Area.

Made in the USA
Thornton, CO
06/06/24 23:23:14

fea2d28a-b0fe-4543-9407-5cc33606c16dR01